THE UNITED STATES
HOW THEY LIVE AND WORK

The United States
HOW THEY LIVE AND WORK

Margaret R. Smith
David M. Smith

DAVID & CHARLES : NEWTON ABBOT

ISBN 0 7153 5784 0

Set in 11pt Baskerville, 2pt leaded
and printed in Great Britain by
Latimer Trend & Company Ltd Plymouth
for David & Charles (Holdings) Limited
South Devon House   Newton Abbot   Devon

Contents

List of Illustrations

(*Maps drawn by Glen M. Fish*)

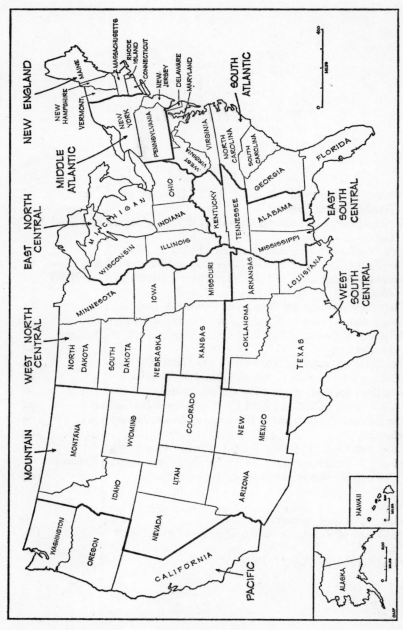

The States, and Regions as defined by the Bureau of the Census.

Introduction

THE Americans are not an easy people to explain, particularly at the present time. The United States is currently in a period of uncertainty and self-evaluation, with traditional attitudes, institutions and national policies being seriously questioned by some people and ardently defended by others. Many of the facts of American life are beyond dispute, but how these are selected, put together and interpreted inevitably involves value judgements and will be to some extent contentious.

The view of how the Americans live and work offered here is a result of six years' residence in the United States, about a quarter of the time spent in travel. It is coloured by the authors' professional experiences as observers and analysts of various aspects of the contemporary national social and economic scene. Acknowledgement is due to the many friends and colleagues who have helped us, wittingly or otherwise, by clarifying facets of American life and national character. Not all of them will agree with our interpretations, but we are sure that we describe an America which they will recognise. We are especially grateful to them for enabling us to take away at least one firm and unalterable impression—that of a singularly warm and hospitable people among whom we have made some of our closest friends.

Throughout this book, the term Americans is used to refer to the inhabitants of the United States. All monetary values are in US dollars ($), which exchange at about $2.40 = £1.00 sterling, and the term 'billion' is used in the American sense of 1,000 million. Most of the figures are from the latest edition of the *Statistical Abstract of the United States* (US Department of Commerce), and relate to the beginning of the 1970s unless otherwise stated.

9

I

The Country and the People

No other people occupy a more crucial position in the modern world than the Americans. The slightest shift in national policy can have almost instantaneous world-wide repercussions, strengthening or threatening the delicate balance of political power or the uncertain stability of the international monetary system. Other nations constantly look to the United States— some with friendliness and expectation, some with hostility and trepidation—recognising that they probably hold the key to the survival of our fragile world civilisation.

Almost 210 million people live in the United States of America. This is roughly 6 per cent of the world's population, and more than in any other nation except China, India and the USSR. The country comprises the forty-eight contiguous states together with the capital of Washington in the District of Columbia, and the two additional states of Hawaii and Alaska. Other territories controlled or administered by the United States include the Canal Zone of Panama, Puerto Rico, Guam, the Virgin Islands, and a number of smaller Pacific and Caribbean islands.

The United States has a total area of about 3,600,000 square miles. It measures almost 4,000 miles west to east from the Pacific Ocean to the coast of Maine, and roughly 1,400 to 1,800 miles north to south between the Canadian and Mexican borders. If a map of the United States (without Alaska) was placed on one of Europe including the eastern USSR, the country would stretch from Ireland to the Ural Mountains and from the Baltic to the Mediterranean and Black Seas. The overall population density is 56 per square mile (roughly the same as Switzerland), or 65 if Alaska is left out, compared with 240 in Europe excluding the USSR. The United States is thus a vast country, densely settled in some areas but very sparsely populated in others—the product of a development process largely confined to the last two centuries.

THE MAKING OF THE UNITED STATES

The first Americans probably arrived in what is now the United States about 15,000 years ago. They came from Asia and crossed into Alaska over a land bridge occupying the present Bering Strait. Many of them gradually moved southwards and eventually reached South America, leaving behind the ancestors of the present Eskimos and other North American Indian tribes.

The North American continent appears to have been first sighted by Europeans in about AD 1000, when Lief Ericson's boat went off course on a voyage from Norway to Greenland. He called it Vinland, and a land of this name to the west of Greenland is marked on a map drawn well before the days of Christopher Columbus. But despite this and other subsequent voyages which took Norsemen to American shores, it was the end of the fifteenth century before Columbus explored the Caribbean and Cabot sailed the north-east coast, to awaken European interest in this New World. In 1507 the erroneous impression that Columbus had reached the East Indies was corrected by naming the new land America, after the Italian explorer Amerigo Vespucci. Further penetrations of this unknown and unexpected continent soon followed, taking the intrepid Spaniards into the southern and south-western interior as well as along the coasts of Florida and the Gulf of Mexico.

The first permanent European settlement in America was at St Augustine on the northern Florida Atlantic coast, established by Spain in 1565. Both the French and the English made attempts at colonisation before the end of the century, but it was 1607 before the first permanent English settlement began at

Jamestown, Virginia. And it was 1620 before the most famous of the early settlers—the Pilgrim Fathers—landed at Plymouth, Massachusetts, in what later became New England.

At the time of the first European settlements, there were about one million Indians living in the territory which is now the United States. Whatever their reaction to the pale-faced newcomers, their occupancy of the land which the Europeans wanted was bound to make them enemies sooner or later, and they were eventually killed in large numbers.

The leading European powers were soon struggling among themselves for the riches of the new continent. Spain extended its influence up the Californian coast and well into the southwest, from its Mexican base. France was soon empire-building in Quebec, and challenging Spain in parts of the south. The Dutch colonised Manhattan Island in the 1620s, built New Amsterdam where New York eventually grew, and expressed their aspirations in the name of New Netherlands. But it was from the small English footholds along the Atlantic coast that the new American nation was to emerge.

By 1700 there were about a quarter of a million English settlers, living in thirteen colonies which extended from Maine southwards to Georgia. By the middle of the eighteenth century the population exceeded 1 million. The growing conflict between the colonies and the British crown came to a head in the famous 'Boston teaparty' of 1773, when a shipload of tea was dumped into the harbour as a protest against import taxes. This heralded the War of Independence, the casting off of British rule, and the birth of the loose confederation of independent colonies which became the first United States.

The growth of the thirteen colonies had been closely associated with Britain's economic strength and sea-power ascendency. The Declaration of Independence in 1776, and the colonists' demonstrated capacity to enforce it, broke the trans-Atlantic political ties but not the vital trade links. Much of the cultural and legal tradition of the 'old country' also survived, and it was men speaking English, rather than Spanish, French or Dutch, who extended the new nation across the continent.

The thirteen colonies and the territories which they claimed at the time of the American Revolution covered most of the land east of the Mississippi River. In 1803 the Louisiana Territory purchased from France added to the nation most of the land between the Mississippi and the Rockies. Florida was acquired from Spain in 1819. Texas was annexed in 1845, and by the middle of the century the remaining land to the west had been ceded by Britain and Spain to take the national territory to the Pacific coast. As new territories were settled and organised into states they could apply for admission to the Union, a process which was completed only sixty years ago with the bestowal of statehood on Arizona and New Mexico in 1912. Outside the coterminous forty-eight states, Alaska was purchased from Russia in 1867 and in 1898 the Hawaiian Islands were annexed. In 1959 Alaska and Hawaii became respectively the forty-ninth and fiftieth states of the Union.

The settlement of the new nation was assisted by improved transportation, and encouraged by the demands of the emerging industrial economy. But the main stimulus was population growth. The first census, taken in 1790 shortly after independence, counted almost 4 million Americans; this had risen to 23 million by the middle of the nineteenth century, and over 70 million by 1900. A particularly important element in this growth was the rising tide of immigration from Europe, as the United States became a haven for the 'huddled masses yearning to breathe free', and a melting pot of people of varied nationality, ethnic origin and religious affiliation. Some joined the swelling city populations, with their distinctive local communities of Italians, Irish, Jews, Germans, Poles, and so on. Others went west in search of land, gold, and other real or illusory opportunities for a new life.

The opening up of the interior would have been virtually impossible without some improvement on the waggon trails which were the main form of transportation until well into the nineteenth century. The first major penetrations were achieved by river, as the broad Mississippi and Ohio took steamboats into the mid-west from the 1820s onwards. Then came the

canals, which helped in the development of the southern hinter-
land of the Great Lakes—the embryonic industrial heartland
of the nation. Railroad building dominated the second half of
the century, as some of the cities were connected up and com-
peting companies raced each other to the Pacific, pulling the
settlement frontier with them.

The rapidly growing population created an enormous market
for food, materials, and consumer goods. As settlement moved
west the farms, mines and lumber camps shipped their products
back along the new river routes, canals and railroads to the
expanding industrial cities in the east, and later developed their
own industrial and service activities. The second half of the
nineteenth century thus saw the growth of various forms of
manufacturing and processing, stimulating each other in an
industrial revolution as great as that which Europe had recently
experienced.

The only major event of the century to divert national energy
from the settling of the land and the exploitation of its resources
was the American Civil War (1861–5). This was the culmina-
tion of a growing division between the northern and southern
states, mainly focused on the slavery which formed the basis of
the plantation economy in the South. The victory of the Union
(North) over the Confederacy (South) brought the nominal
freeing of millions of Negro slaves. But the war also had less
fortunate consequences: the economy of the South took decades
to recover, and defeat left a scar which some of its people still
express in an exaggerated pride in their southernness, in displays
of the old Confederacy flag, and in a general distrust of northern
'Yankees'.

The process of man firmly implanting himself on the American landscape has continued at a rapidly accelerating pace
through the present century. Recent years have seen dramatic
developments, as the metropolitan suburbs spread across the
countryside, concrete multi-lane highways funnel commuters
into the central business districts and connect up the cities, and
the airports expand to occupy more land than most cities did
a few years ago. Ever larger industrial plants are built on the

fringe of the cities and along the highways, rivers and coasts, while hotels, apartment blocks and retirement or vacation homes line the best of the beaches and lake shores. And the development of the land is still far from complete.

The way in which the land was settled and the economy developed is of major importance in understanding the Americans. With very little guidance and control from the national or state governments, and with personal gain as the main motivating force, resources were often exploited thoughtlessly and without regard to the long-term economic and ecological consequences. The land was limited and its resources finite, however, and the full price of the destroyed forests, the lost soil, and the polluted air and water is still being exacted today.

The American nation was built by an energetic people, imposing themselves with strength on a rich yet hostile land, and the process has left a deep imprint on the character and values of their successors. It helps to explain the rugged individualism of the frontier people, which contemporary Americans revere and try to emulate; the national preoccupation with guns and other symbols of masculinity, and the readiness to solve personal and national problems by the use of force; the exploitive view of natural resources, and a need to dominate or even replace nature rather than come to terms with it; the attitude to the ownership of land, including the high value attached to the freedom of the owner to develop it how he wishes; the belief in competition, and the arrogance which often accompanies hard-won economic or political success; and the lack of sympathy for the weak and unsuccessful, who would have been a serious social liability on the frontier. And it also helps to explain the tradition of self-help and self-sufficiency developed when survival depended on the collective strength of the family and the local community rather than on the remote power of the government, in days when the cavalry did not always arrive in time.

THE LAND AND ITS RESOURCES

For the United States to become the world's leading industrial nation less than four centuries after its first European settlement required more than an enterprising and energetic people. It also required a land of rich resources.

Three major features dominate the physical make-up of the United States: (1) the massive western mountain ranges extending from Alaska to Mexico and including the Rockies; (2) the narrower and smaller Appalachian Mountains in the east; and (3) the great central plains formed by the basin of the Mississippi River and its tributaries. Initially the two mountainous regions posed problems for communications and settlement, and for long were regarded as liabilities rather than assets. The Appalachians contained the early colonists in their Atlantic coastal enclaves until their passes were discovered and trails pushed through. The western ranges for centuries isolated the Pacific coastal settlements started by the Spanish missionaries and stimulated by the gold rushes and growing trade of the nineteenth century. But when men finally moved into them, the mountains proved rich in minerals. In the Appalachian valleys coal and iron ore provided the basis for the heavy industries of Pennsylvania and elsewhere, which fed their pig-iron and steel to the growing engineering and metal-goods industries. The Rockies and the ranges to the west yielded a variety of non-ferrous minerals—silver and gold, copper and lead, potash and sulphur—to provide materials for other industrial activities. The wealth of the mountains also included their vast forests, their building stone and their streams, which could be harnessed to drive waterwheels and later generate electricity.

The main resource of the plains was their soil. From the intensively worked farmlands of Europe the settlers came to what must have seemed an almost endless expanse of virgin land, and if in places it proved unsuitable for a particular crop

B

it could generally be put to other profitable use. But it had to be treated with care, as was shown by the soil erosion and the 'dust bowls' of the 1930s when the wind blew away the exposed topsoil from thousands of acres in Oklahoma and other parts of the southern plains. Other resources lay beneath the soil— enough oil and natural gas eventually to sustain the fuel requirements of a multiplicity of industrial and domestic uses.

Flanking the Appalachians on their east and south were the coastal lowlands. These were sufficiently extensive to provide good land for the agricultural economy of the early colonies, some materials for small-scale industry, and sites for the fishing harbours, ports and trading centres which eventually developed into such cities as Boston, New York, Philadelphia, Baltimore and New Orleans. The west coast was less inviting, comprising low mountain ranges for the most part. But there were places where settlements could grow into Los Angeles, San Francisco and Seattle, and between the coastal ranges and the Sierra Nevada lay the rich Central Valley of California.

Major rivers and their valleys provided access to the interior, but none was to prove as important as the Great Lakes. These comprised, in effect, a series of inland seas, which offered relatively cheap water transportation into the heart of the continent along the major industrial axis from New England to the mid-west. Like the rivers, the lakes also provided somewhere for the growing cities to dump their sewage and the industries their effluence.

The development of America's varied agricultural economy, which provides industries with raw materials as well as people with food, was greatly assisted by climatic conditions. These range from sub-tropical in Florida to cool temperate in the Pacific north-west and to a Mediterranean type in part of California. The extremes are represented by the dry heat of the south-western deserts, and the bitter cold and deep snows of winter in the Rockies and upper plains. Annual rainfall varies from over 50 inches in parts of the South to virtually nil in some of the south-western basins and ranges. Summer daytime temperatures exceed 90°F in most of the southern half of the country but are below 70°F along much of the Pacific coast. In winter the range is from well below zero in the northern plains and parts of the Rockies to over 60°F in southern Florida. The average annual hours of sunshine ranges from over 4,000 in California's Mojave Desert to less than 2,000 in the extreme north-west. The frost-free season is less than 100 days in parts of the western mountains and little more in the northern plains, but it rises to over 300 in Florida, parts of the Gulf Coast, and the southern extremity of California. The growing season varies from less than 200 days in the northern mountains and plains to 365 days in a strip along the country's southern border from California to South Carolina. Alaska and Hawaii have their own distinctive climates.

Local and regional agricultural specialisation can be attributed partly to combinations of favourable climatic and soil conditions. In the South, for example, the exacting requirements of cotton cultivation are met, and the same is true for corn (maize) in the mid-west. The warmth of southern California and Florida helps to produce varied fruit and vegetables, and rice can be grown in the Mississippi delta. Improvements in technology are pushing farming into areas where the resources of the land have previously been underdeveloped because of climatic shortcomings; examples are the Columbia Basin in Washington and parts of the Mojave Desert and the Imperial Valley in California, where the Grand Coulee and Hoover Dams have made possible the controlled use of water for irrigation.

Not all America's land and natural resources are bonded in service to the economy. The way in which the national territory was expanded in the nineteenth century led to government ownership of large areas of land and one-third of the total surface area of the United States is still in federal hands. Most of this is under the control of the Department of the Interior, and includes the National Parks and other areas protected from economic development.

The use of land and water for recreation is important to the American people. They have some of the greatest scenic wonders of the world, including the Grand Canyon, the peaks of the Rockies, Carlsbad Caverns, the Alaskan glaciers, the Hawaiian and Aleutian volcanoes, the swamps of Florida's Everglades, and the quiet bayous of the Louisiana coast. There are also relics of the pre-Columbian Indian culture, such as the cliff dwellings of the south-west. It is a tribute to the foresight of a few individuals that so many areas of outstanding natural beauty and historic interest were protected from the land grabs of the nineteenth and early twentieth centuries, and consequent despoilation or destruction.

A COUNTRY OF CONTRASTS

The nature of the land and the way it has been settled and developed have made the United States a country of contrasts.

The most common view of the United States is probably that of mid-century metropolitan America—the world of the travelling businessman, the well-to-do vacationer, and the mass of the middle classes. It is made up of bustling airports, smart motels, and fast Interstate Highways cutting through expansive wheatfields or forests with their crop neatly lined up to await the mechanical harvester or saw. In the city it is characterised by the suburban ranch-style bungalow homes, the brash modern shopping centres or 'malls' with their vast carparks of wall-to-wall tarmac, the multi-lane freeways into the business district, the gleaming concrete-and-glass office blocks of the great corporations or departments of government, and the flashing neon signs of 'fast-food joints' and night spots. It is a world which exudes newness, efficiency, and high technological and economic achievement.

But there is another America, the reverse image. This is the America of the sideroads away from the Interstates—a land of small towns selling supplies to farmers, of fishing hamlets on rocky coasts, of wooden shacks in the rural South beside decaying plantation houses, of crumbling mining towns in the Rockies or an isolated Appalachian valley, and of the solitude of the back country and the wilderness. In the cities it is the squalid slums barely visible to the freeway commuter, the ghetto and 'skid row', the monotonous bungalows of the blue-collar workers, acres of factories pouring their pollutants into the air and water, and the dying downtown area losing its business to the suburbs.

Each region has its own distinctive landscape and character. New England is a land of small farms and fishing villages, with white-painted wooden houses against a green back-cloth of fields and forests. Little towns with English names serve the countryside, while to the south, towards the city of Boston, are nineteenth-century redbrick cotton-mill towns which might almost have been transplanted from Lancashire. In Connecticut the growing New York suburbs extend eastwards along the routes of the commuter railroads and fast turnpike roads.

New York is unlike any other city on earth. The Manhattan skyscrapers, seen on one of the few days with clean air, or at night as a group of fragile illuminated boxes, must be one of the most dramatic sights of the man-made world. In the inner suburbs massive apartment complexes compete with commercial buildings, highways and cemeteries for the limited land, and the outer suburbs of the middle classes spread steadily into the countryside. There is the misery of the Harlem ghetto, and some of the finest museums and galleries anywhere. To many visitors and newcomers, New York is a hostile city from the first encounter with a cab driver or porter; to others it has a warmth and vitality which make it the only place where they would ever consider living.

The Appalachian Mountains form a series of long ridges separating deep valleys often hidden in haze. Names like the Alleghenys and the Cumberland Gap evoke the struggles of the early settlers to cross this barrier. Today the Appalachians form one of the major depressed regions of the United States, with poor 'hillbilly' farmers and miners living in hollows between the hills torn apart by the big mining corporations as they took out the coal for industry elsewhere.

In the South the popular image of vast plantations run from

beautiful ante-bellum mansions set in azalia gardens obscures the sad reality of rural poverty. In the cities, not far from the new office blocks of Atlanta and Birmingham, the refineries and space laboratories of the Gulf Coast, and the luxury hotels of Miami Beach, there are ghettos where social conditions are as bad as anywhere in the nation. The South is heavily wooded, with the plantations of the lumber company now more prominent than those of the cotton grower.

The Great Plains are almost endless expanses of wheat prairies, cornfields and cattle ranches. The main cities appear as skyscraper oases, with their commercial centres, stockyards and railroad termini funnelling the farm produce to the nation's food markets. This is a region of small towns which never grew, with a group of grain elevators along the railroad track, a dusty Main Street built optimistically wide and long where the shops peter out after a couple of blocks, and a small and uninviting hotel on the corner where the Greyhound bus stops each day. The population is declining in much of the plains.

The Great Plains gradually rise to the edge of the Rockies—a stark ridge of grey peaks and snowy caps. Beyond are the dry basins and tablelands, with mesas and buttes, and the sand-and-rock landscape of the Western movie. It is a land of ghost towns of the mining booms with names like Cripple Creek and Rawhide, of Indians scratching a living out of their infertile reservations, of beautiful emptiness, and of the gambling and nightlife oases of Reno and Las Vegas. Here is the searing heat of Death Valley and the Mojave Desert, and places called Stovepipe Wells and Twentynine Palms.

On the west coast is California. Built on the prosperity of modern technology applied to the manufacture of aircraft and electronic equipment and to the tilling of the soil, the cities of California epitomise the achievements and nightmares of mid-century America. Los Angeles spreads out across its basin into the adjoining hills like a formless urban amoeba with its freeway lifelines, in an almost perpetual haze of polluted air. Here the successful realise the full 'American dream', with luxury houses and private pools in Beverly Hills or some other exclusive suburb and never quite enough cars, boats, television sets and the like to stop them striving for more. And it is here that the Watts riots erupted in 1965, in a cry of anguish soon echoed in city ghettos across the country as the deprived black populations found a new and frightening outlet for their anger and frustration. San Francisco, with its Golden Gate Bridge, Chinatown, and Fisherman's Wharf, is quite different. Like Los Angeles it has its extremes of poverty and affluence and its monotonous suburbs, but it is surrounded on three sides by water and has a cosmopolitan atmosphere which makes it for many people their favourite American city. Across the San Francisco Bay is Berkeley, where the modern era of student dissent was born and where the city council is now controlled by radicals, in a state with a conservative former film star as governor. In this country of contrasts, California contains something of all the extremes.

POPULATION

From the time of the Pilgrim Fathers it took three centuries for the population of the United States to reach 100 million. The second 100 million took only fifty years, and during the present century the population has risen from 75 million to almost 210 million. The increase in the 1960s alone was little short of 25 million. Rapid population growth is one of the important realities of American life.

Equally important is the urbanisation of the American people. The transition from an agricultural to an industrial economy changed them from a largely rural people to predominantly city dwellers; the first American census (1790) showed only one person in twenty living in a city with over 2,500 inhabitants, whereas today it is almost three out of four. So despite the vast size of the country and the spread of settlement during the last century, the American population is still highly concentrated geographically.

The largest concentration is in the east, in the belt extending from Boston through New York and on to Baltimore and Washington DC. This is the area sometimes called 'Megalopolis', in recognition of its gradual coalescence of individual cities, satellites and suburbs to form an almost continuous urban region 400 miles long. Similar megalopolitan tendencies can be detected elsewhere, centred on Detroit and Chicago in the north and on Los Angeles and San Francisco in the west.

To many Americans the everyday environment is thus that of the major city and its suburbs. The fifty largest cities alone account for a total of 40 million people, or almost one in five of all Americans. The 1970 Census recorded six cities with over a million people: New York (7,868,000), Chicago (3,367,000), Los Angeles (2,816,000), Philadelphia (1,949,000), Detroit (1,511,000) and Houston (1,233,000). However, these figures do not include all the suburbs which are geographically part of the greater metropolitan areas; the population of the entire New York metropolitan area, for example, now approaches 12 million. Between 1960 and 1970 the national suburban population grew by more than 25 per cent, while the population of the central or inner-city areas went up by less than 10 per cent.

The 1970 Census provides an up-to-date view of the population, and how it is changing. The Americans are a young people, and getting younger, with half the population under 28 years of age and more than a quarter under 15. The fastest growth in the 1960s was in the 15–24 age group, as the immediate post-war 'baby boom' reached adolescence and adulthood. But there are also many old people; one American in ten is over 65, and the increase in this age group since 1960 has been 20 per cent. The non-white population rose by over 20 per cent between 1960 and 1970, compared with 12 per cent for whites. The number of women increased slightly faster than the number of men; women have been in the majority in the United States since the end of World War II. The total population of almost 208 million in 1970 in the United States and outlying areas includes over 3 million in Puerto Rico and other possessions, and 1.7 million Americans abroad in the armed forces and other government service (including families).

The Americans are a mobile people, changing their place of residence on average once every five years. The 1970 Census shows a continuing movement to the cities and away from the countryside, and there has been a marked shift from the interior towards the sea coasts, with Florida and California as the major targets. About one-third of the 3,000 or so counties have lost population for the past three decades, most of them in a broad band extending through the Great Plains from the Canadian to the Mexican border and reaching from there across much of the rural South. On balance the population has continued its historic tendency to move west, and its 'centre of gravity', as calculated by the Bureau of the Census, has shifted from Terre Haute, Indiana, in 1940, to a position in Illinois about 30 miles east of St Louis. By the next census, the centre of population should have crossed the Mississippi for the first time.

The birth rate in the United States has fallen steadily throughout the present century, except for the immediate post-war years. It is now almost down to 17 per 1,000 population (slightly above the UK and the USSR but less than half that of some nations), compared with 30 in 1910, but this still means over 3.5 million babies each year. Life expectancy at birth is now almost 75 for white females (55 in 1920) and 67 for white males (54 in 1920), while for non-white females it is 68 (45 in 1920) and for males 60 (45 in 1920).

Despite a marked decrease in the birth rate at the beginning of the 1970s, the continuing growth of population is causing concern because of pressure on limited natural resources. The increasing metropolitan concentration also poses problems of city planning, congestion and environmental pollution.

RACIAL AND ETHNIC ORIGINS

The American population is made up of persons with a wide range of national origins and racial or ethnic characteristics. In the past 150 years more than 45 million immigrants have entered the country, almost 6 million of them during the last twenty years. The largest numbers have come from Germany (6.9m), Italy (5.2m), Great Britain (4.8m), Ireland (4.7m), Austria and Hungary (4.3m), Canada (4.0m), and Russia (3.3m). Uncounted millions were also imported from Africa as slaves. Today's steady stream of immigrants contains representatives of European nations, but Mexico and Canada are now the leading sources.

The most conspicuous of the American minority groups are the Blacks (a name now often preferred to Negroes). There are almost 23 million black Americans, making up one in eight of the total population. Demographically the Blacks differ from the Whites in having higher birthrates, higher infant mortality, lower life expectancy, and more fatherless families. Blacks differ also in their geographical distribution, being mainly concentrated in the South and the large industrial cities of the northeast and mid-west. One of the major trends in recent years has been the migration of Blacks from the South to the industrial centres of the North. In 1940 just over three-quarters of all Blacks lived in the South, while today the proportion is only about half. The states with the heaviest inflow of Blacks between 1960 and 1970 were New York and California, followed by Illinois, Michigan and New Jersey, while the biggest outflows were from Mississippi, Alabama, the Carolinas and Louisiana. Discussion of the special situation of the Blacks in American society is reserved for Chapter 8, where racial minority problems are examined.

The second largest non-white element in the population is the American Indian. These now number about half a million, most of them living on the reservations of the south-western states. They share some of the social deprivation and special demographic characteristics of the Blacks, but have a few special problems of their own. In addition there are in the United States about 460,000 Japanese, almost 250,000 Chinese and 175,000 Philippinos, heavily concentrated in California and Hawaii.

LANGUAGE

Bernard Shaw once described America and Britain as two nations divided by a common language. In view of the diverse origins of the American people it is not surprising that the English language as they speak it has some distinctive features, as well as an accent easily recognisable in a Europe well exposed to American movies, television dramas, servicemen and tourists.

The language spoken and written in the United States, though very close to that of Britain in vocabulary and syntax, does contain some grammatical variations on the Queen's English. This may be partly because the writing of English prose is an accomplishment not greatly emphasised in many American schools. But it is largely due to the imperfect mastering of the English language by immigrants from Europe. Distortions of the standard form of the language are, as elsewhere, very common among the less educated, and this is especially true of the poorer Blacks. Words from the languages of the immigrants have found their way into American English, though they appear colloquially more often than in print. There are also some English words which have a different meaning in America.

Last century it was common for first-generation immigrants to continue the use of their native language as far as possible. This was often encouraged in the home as a means of preserving national identity and links with the 'old country'. But this gradually changed as the second generation went to school, and pressure towards conformity meant denial of the old language. Foreign languages are still used locally—for example, French in parts of southern Louisiana and a form of German in the 'Pennsylvania Dutch' country, and some cities still publish foreign language newspapers. The most common language other than English today is the Spanish spoken by Mexican immigrants in the south-west, by the many Cubans in Miami, and by the Puerto Ricans in Spanish Harlem. Some indigenous Indian languages are retained on the reservations.

Like the English spoken in Britain, colloquial American contains many expressions originating in sport. 'Taking a rain check' on an invitation means putting it off to be taken up later, from the practice in baseball of issuing a ticket for a later game to spectators at one which has been rained off. 'Pinch hitting' for someone means taking his place, from the batter in baseball who substitutes for the pitcher. Making calls on a number of people is 'touching bases', and an expected outcome would be 'par for the course'.

As in other countries, currency has its own slang. A five-cent piece is a 'nickel', ten cents a 'dime', twenty-five cents is a 'quarter' (also two 'bits'), and a dollar (100 cents) is a 'buck'. The fact that $1,000 is a 'grand' will have escaped few readers of American cops-and-robbers fiction. American paper currency of all denominations is the same size and has the same grey tones on the front and green on the back—hence banknotes are 'greenbacks'.

RELIGION

Religious practice has always been important for the bulk of the American people. It was the search for freedom to worship as they wished which took the Pilgrims across the Atlantic, and subsequent phases of immigration involved large numbers of Irish Catholics and European Jews as well as adherents to various Protestant churches. They were certainly not all escaping religious persecution, but their faith was a major element of national or ethnic identity which they generally expected to retain in the United States. Added to those which the immigrants brought with them are religions indigenous to America or which first took real shape there—the Christian Scientists, the Church of Jesus Christ of Latter Day Saints (the Mormons), and a number of evangelical and fundamentalist sects.

The contribution of the Blacks to American religious life provides another diverse element. Whatever beliefs they brought

from Africa soon disappeared in the days of slavery, for they
were discouraged from adhering to old faiths, and were expected to adopt the religion of the Whites. But they did bring
to the churches an emotionalism and vitality of their own, as
expressed in the Negro spiritual and in special congregational
participation in the service. In recent years the Black Muslim
church has become quite prominent in some cities, offering a
religion with more emphasis on Black and African identity.

Some of the traditional religions of the indigenous peoples of
America are preserved on the Indian reservations. They are
expressed in dances and other colourful ceremonials, and in
ancient rites performed in the privacy of the underground
kiva.

Religious diversity and freedom are thus a predictable outcome of the way America developed. The constitutional separation of Church and State means that no single denomination
has a formally recognized position of privilege, as is usual in
European countries. But all are not necessarily equal. For
example, some status attaches to being a WASP (White Anglo-
Saxon Protestant), with its implication of a desirable combination of skin colour, ethnic origin, and religious affiliation. Until
the election of John Kennedy in 1960 there were doubts as to
whether a Catholic could ever become President, and some
discrimination has been the unfortunate experience of Jews in
the United States, as elsewhere.

Churchgoing is more prevalent in the United States than in
Britain. The National Council of Churches recently estimated
that 60 per cent of the population regularly attends church or
synagogue. The largest group is the Roman Catholic Church
with well over 30 million members, followed by the Baptists
with about 25 million and the Methodists with 17 million. Then
come the Lutheran, Jewish, Episcopalian, Presbyterian and
Mormon churches.

Almost every major religious group in America has links with
some comparable denomination in Europe. Although forms of
worship may be similar, American churches have their own
atmosphere and ritual, which at the extreme can make them

quite unlike those of other countries. In some of the fundamentalist sects of the southern 'Bible Belt', where the strict
interpretation of the Scriptures is an important article of faith,
the service can become an uninhibited expression of emotion
as the preacher works himself up into a frenzy of oratory and
his congregation respond.

Just as in Europe, some churches in the United States can
provide entrée to business success and social status. To quote
from Erskine Caldwell's *Deep South*: 'For the wealthy, a membership in one of the fashionable Protestant churches is the best
investment in town—tax deductible, with superior business
contacts, high rank in local society, and automatic salvation.'

Certain facets of American religion have become big business,
so important are they to certain segments of the population.
There are a number of millionaire preachers, and some pseudo-
religious colleges which sell ordinations and theology degrees.
Revival meetings, 'old-time' religion and gospel music all have
ardent followings, often backed by commercial promoters.

In general, religious faith is an important and constructive
thread in the fabric of many aspects of American life. Church
membership is a major source of strength in individual and
family life, and a motivating force for philanthropic actions at
home and abroad. Belief in God and a fervent patriotic faith
in the American way of life are closely intertwined, and are
expressed in the idea of the 'manifest destiny' of the United
States as a world power and major force for good against evil.

The Puritan tradition of some of the early immigrants is still
influential in American life, for example, in attitudes to alcohol
and sex. So is the Protestant ethic of hard work and self-help.
The religious beliefs so deeply imbedded in the American social
and economic system help to explain the importance attached
to individual effort and voluntary community actions, and
ambivalent attitudes to government welfare schemes and the
treatment of society's weaker brethren.

THE AMERICAN CHARACTER

The way the nation came into being was bound to make the Americans a highly distinctive people. Despite the diversity of racial and ethnic origin, homogeneity and conformity characterise many aspects of contemporary life. The American character, in so far as such a thing can be identified, comprises a unique blend of varied cultural traditions, tempered by the experiences of a new environment and by the requirements of a new national identity.

To say that the Americans are a people of paradoxes is trite but true. They are a forward-looking people with a fascination for technological gymnastics, yet with extreme reverence for the past and a nostalgia for the hard simplicity of the pioneering days. They will tear down buildings of distinguished architecture and cover field after field with concrete suburbs and tarmac car parks, yet they are devoted to their national battlefields and monuments almost as to temples of patriotism. They see themselves as the heirs of men of the frontiers and the backwoods, yet seek nature and the great outdoors in air-conditioned cars and caravans and eat more processed food than any nation on earth. They pride themselves on their rugged individualism, yet submit to powerful forces for conformity from the cradle to the grave and regard anyone conspicuously different with suspicion. They claim to be hard-headed financial realists, yet they will spend their money on almost any new gadget.

Their country was born with the rejection of the British monarchy, and they still bestow no titles or nobility on their leading citizens. Yet they yearn for status, expressing it in an ostentatious display of Cadillacs, yachts, expensive houses, and other material symbols of wealth and success. They claim to be classless, yet in some of the older cities there exists a real aristocracy, and there is a strong element of class conflict in racial discrimination and prejudice. As in Europe, social status can derive solely from family identity, as for example with the older wealthy families of the east, and with the Daughters of the American Revolution who all trace their ancestry back to soldiers of the War of Independence. However, high social position is generally accompanied by wealth and political power, the former often purchasing the latter.

Many of the apparent paradoxes are not hard to explain. The United States is a pluralistic society, with conflicting interests, aspirations and values. The concept of equality conflicts with the differentiation of the successful, going 'back to nature' is inconsistent with the preservation of creature comforts, the aesthetic improvement of the environment conflicts with economic progress, and so on. The simultaneous achievement of mutually exclusive objectives is impossible, but this is exactly what the Americans are often led to attempt.

This is in turn related to national idealism. By their very nature ideals are seldom if ever attained, and the higher the ideals the more obvious the gap which separates them from reality. In a society which describes itself as 'the land of the free' and 'the bastion of democracy', the curtailment of personal freedom or the distortion of the democratic process will attract more attention than in a nation which makes no claims to perfection. A further factor is that such grand abstractions as

---

Winter in Yosemite Park, a protected area of outstanding natural beauty in California's Sierra Nevada.

A pineapple plantation in Hawaii: modern methods of cultivation developed with the help of the US Department of Agriculture's Soil Conservation Service.

freedom, liberty, equality and justice, while almost universally
accepted as desirable, are subject to a variety of interpretations.
For example, freedom to one American may mean being able
to build a factory where he pleases, but for another it may be
the capacity to breathe clean air and have a pleasant view from
his home. Social justice to one may mean payment by results,
to another it may mean payment according to need.

Thus the Americans claim to be egalitarian, yet strive to become unequal. They value individual freedom, yet are quite
capable of infringing the freedom of those with whom they disagree. They advocate law and order, yet much business is
conducted from a precarious position on the edge of illegality.
They place high value on justice, yet are reluctant to extend
some of its provisions to the poor and the black. Their collective
generosity is expressed in enormous expenditures on foreign
aid and individually they are capable of great compassion and
personal goodwill, yet as a nation they can perpetrate and
rationalise war crimes in Vietnam and be largely indifferent
to the suffering of their own underprivileged people.

But if in America the realities of life depart from the ideal,
so they do in every country on earth. The ideals are truly great
ones, and in so many aspects of national life no other country

---

New York's skyscrapers, looking north-east from the top of the
Empire State Building.

San Francisco, with its docks, warehouses, freeways and offices.

can point to the kind of progress made in the United States. It is easy to overlook this in these times of critical national self-evaluation.

However the country looks to outsiders, and to the dissidents within, most Americans appear well satisfied with it. Above all else, they are a patriotic people. They may at times show a sense of inferiority or insecurity, which can find expression in brash or over-assertive behaviour. And they have a tendency to look with envy at some features of the more mature nations of Europe, and with unconcealed awe at holders of the titled nobility which they deny themselves. They are a young country and often show it, but there is no lack of pride in being themselves.

They have no monarchy, but they do have their flag. It is the most important symbol of national identity, its fifty stars representing the states and its thirteen stripes the original colonies. The flag is treated with great deference, and penalties attach to its defacement or improper use. It is flown frequently and with evident pride, and allegiance is pledged to the flag rather than to any personage. The office of the President is greatly respected, even when the incumbent is not, but this is not the same as the feeling for the flag.

In these days of dissent and social activism, the flag is very much a symbol of believing in America and of faith in its traditional institutions and values. It is appearing with increasing frequency in automobile windows, on the sleeves of policemen, and elsewhere, as a clear statement of anti-radical political sentiment. Stickers on automobile bumpers will also proclaim 'I am Proud to be an American', 'My Country—Right or Wrong', and 'America—Love it or Leave it'. They do love it, they are genuinely proud to be a part of it, and they sincerely believe that it is the greatest country on earth.

2

How the Country is Run

WHEN the original colonies gained their independence from Britain, they faced the immediate problem of how they would govern themselves. In 1787 representatives of the thirteen new states (except Rhode Island) met in Philadelphia to settle this issue, and the outcome was the Constitution of the United States. This document has subsequently been widely recognised as a model blueprint for democratic government, and was once described by W. E. Gladstone as 'the most wonderful work ever struck off at a given time by the brain and purpose of man'.

The purpose of American government, as expressed in the preamble to the Constitution, is 'to form a more perfect Union, establish Justice, insure domestic Tranquility, provide for the common defense, promote the general Welfare and secure the Blessings of Liberty to ourselves and our Posterity'. The Constitution represented a unique application of a long cultural and legal tradition to the special circumstances of the New World. The 'Founding Fathers' who wrote it were aware of centuries of accumulated English experience in matters of government, and were also influenced by the contemporary European debate over political philosophy in an age of intellectual enlightenment and growing social idealism. They were wise and experienced men, and they chose their words with care. The form of government which they created has served their successors well, proving firm enough to maintain the stability of a growing nation through most of two turbulent centuries, yet flexible enough to adapt to changing circumstances.

THE CONSTITUTION

The Constitution is the keystone of the American system of government. Since it was written there have been twenty-six Amendments, including the ten in the Bill of Rights ratified in 1791 and virtually part of the original. Most of the Amendments have involved additions and clarification of definitions, the only fundamental changes being in the 13th (1865), which abolished slavery and the 19th (1920), which enfranchised women. Only one has been repealed—the 18th (prohibition), repealed by the 21st in 1933. The Constitution has three main features: it grants and limits the powers of the national and state governments, it expresses the liberties of the people (including freedom of religion, of speech and of the press), and it establishes a federal government with the separation of power between three branches.

The Constitution is very specific about the distribution of power between the federal and state governments. The states may control elections, local government, public health, safety and morals, within their boundaries. This includes such matters as marriage, divorce, education, voting qualifications, and commerce within the state. The states may not intervene in the major functions of the federal government, such as making war, signing treaties with foreign countries, maintaining armies or navies, and printing currency.

The federal government may regulate commerce between two or more states and with foreign nations, ratify treaties, and conduct foreign relations. It may establish rules of bankruptcy, maintain post offices and post roads, grant patents and copyrights, coin money and regulate its value, declare war, and raise, support and make rules relating to an army or navy. The federal government may not favour one state over another, grant titles of nobility, or suspend habeas corpus except in cases of rebellion or invasion.

Both state and federal governments may levy taxes, build

roads, borrow money, and spend money for the general welfare. Neither may deprive persons of life or property without due process of law, or pass laws incriminating people for acts not illegal when committed.

The Bill of Rights added the first ten Amendments to the Constitution, clarifying the liberties of the people. Under it, the people are granted the following rights:

to assemble peaceably, and to petition Congress;

to keep and bear arms;

not to have soldiers quartered in their homes in peacetime except as prescribed by law;

to be secure against unreasonable searches and seizures;

in general not to be held to answer criminal charges except upon indictment;

not to be put twice in jeopardy for the same offence;

not to be compelled to bear witness against oneself;

not to be deprived of life, liberty, or property without due process of law;

to receive just compensation for private property, taken for public use;

in criminal prosecutions, to be given trial by jury—to be notified of the charges, to be confronted with witnesses, to have compulsory process for calling witnesses, and to have legal counsel;

to have a jury trial in suits at law involving over twenty dollars;

not to have excessive bail required, nor excessive fines imposed, nor cruel and unusual punishment inflicted.

This is the content of the first eight Amendments. The 9th and 10th reserve to the states or the people all powers not delegated to the federal government, or prohibited to them by Constitution.

The Constitution provides for the separation of powers between three branches of federal government: the Executive, the Legislative, and the Judicial. One man is vested with executive power—the President—sworn to 'preserve, protect and defend' the Constitution. Federal legislative powers are vested in the Congress, which comprises the Senate and the House of Representatives. Judicial power is vested in the Supreme Court.

The writers of the Constitution built into the federal government a system of checks and balances. The objective was to prevent any one branch from assuming more than its proper role in the affairs of state. The Executive (the President) may check Congress by vetoing legislation, by recommending legislation, and by calling Congress into special session. It may check the Judiciary by the nomination of judges to the Supreme Court. The Legislative branch (Congress) may check the President by refusing to pass legislation or appropriate funds, by a two-thirds vote overriding his veto, and by the Senate not approving Presidential appointments and not ratifying treaties. Congress may also check the President by impeachment charges, brought by the House of Representatives and heard before the Senate. Congress may check the Judiciary by enacting new laws to replace those held unconstitutional, initiating amendments to the Constitution, decreasing or increasing the number of judges on the Supreme Court, and passing laws defining the jurisdiction of the Federal Courts. Congress itself is checked by requirements that both the House of Representatives and the Senate must pass a bill if it is to become law. The Judiciary (Supreme Court) may check the President by declaring unconstitutional acts of the Executive branch, and it can check the Congress by declaring laws unconstitutional.

It is in this delicate system of checks and balances that much of the strength of the American system is to be found. In practice the executive, legislative and judicial functions of government are not strictly separated, as there are substantial areas of overlap. But there is a dispersal of power, and it is this which provides the ultimate brake on what some political commentators see as an emerging danger in contemporary American government—the growing power of the Executive branch under the President.

THE EXECUTIVE BRANCH

Despite the checks placed on him, the President of the United States is probably the most powerful elected official in the world.

As head of state he has the power to appoint all officers of the government, subject to the approval of the Senate, and he can dismiss them without even recourse to that body. He also appoints all judges and ambassadors. The President has the power to call Congress into special session to declare war, to ratify treaties, or to deal with other crucial matters. He is commander-in-chief of the armed forces. He is leader of his political party. The President can initiate legislation, and he outlines his programme and aspirations at the beginning of each year in the State of the Union Message, which is similar to the Monarch's Speech at the opening of Parliament in Britain.

The President is the one man ultimately responsible for executive government in the United States. He obtains advice from his own personal administrative staff and councillors, from the Departments of State, from the National Security Council, and from the leaders of his own party. He can also call in leaders in the Congress, organised labour, and any other body whose views he wishes to hear on a particular matter. But he is completely free to accept or reject such advice.

The President is elected to a term of four years, and nothing can remove him from office except death, disability or impeachment. He can be re-elected for a second term, but cannot serve more than two complete consecutive terms. The transfer of power from one President to another has to take place at noon on 20 January following the election.

A new President brings with him a new Administration. There is usually a change of staff, from the highest executive to the humblest clerk, and there is thus little continuity of government civil service. The White House staff can and does exert more influence on the President than anyone else. The President appoints his own staff members, usually on the basis of political patronage; for example, many appointees are men who have been with the President during his election campaign and are thus rewarded for loyal and efficient service. They do not have to have any other qualifications or experience, but they will, of course, be people in whose ability the President feels he has good reason to be confident. In addition to the White House staff, the Executive Offices of the President include the Office of Management and Budget, the Council of Economic Advisers, the Council on Environmental Quality, and other offices performing similar specialist functions.

There are twelve Departments of State in the Executive Branch. Each is run by a Presidential appointee, generally with some interest or expertise in the field, and usually but not always a member of the President's own party. These twelve individuals make up the Cabinet. Although some members may be influential advisers to the President, the Cabinet as a body does not share in making top-level decisions to any significant degree.

The Department of State heads comprising the Cabinet are:

    The Secretary of State (foreign affairs)
    The Secretary of the Treasury
    The Secretary of Defense
    The Attorney General (Department of Justice)
    The Postmaster General (United States Postal Service)
    The Secretary of the Interior
    The Secretary of Agriculture
    The Secretary of Commerce
    The Secretary of Labor
    The Secretary of Health, Education and Welfare
    The Secretary of Housing and Urban Development
    The Secretary of Transportation

In addition to the various Executive Offices and Departments of State, there are over thirty independent offices and establishments. These range from the Atomic Energy Commission to the Veterans Administration.

The only elected Member of the Executive Branch apart from the President is the Vice-President. This office is of little real consequence, except that the Vice-President succeeds the President if the latter cannot complete his term, as when Lyndon Johnson became President on the death of John Kennedy. The prospective Vice-President stands for election with the Presidential candidate, and great care has to be taken in his selection. He is often chosen to balance the 'ticket'; for example, if the Presidential candidate is a northern liberal there might be an attempt to get a southerner of more conservative persuasion as his 'running mate'. The Vice-President represents the President in a number of capacities, but has virtually no power of his own. His chief official duty is to preside in the Senate.

Neither the President nor his Cabinet members sit in Congress. Public discussion between the President and Congress and between the President and the general public is usually conducted through the mass media, the official responsible for arranging this being the White House Press Secretary. The President holds press conferences, which are often televised, and the Press is always in attendance at the White House and on Presidential travels. The use of television for talking directly to the American people is an increasingly popular means of communication for the President.

The White House in Washington DC is the President's official residence, though he may maintain private homes elsewhere. For his onerous duties he gets paid $200,000 each year. He is formally referred to as 'Mr President', and his family is treated with a similar respect to that afforded to the family of monarchs in Europe.

THE LEGISLATIVE BRANCH

The Congress of the United States is the body in which the Constitution vests federal legislative power. Congress is divided into two houses—the Senate and the House of Representatives. In the Senate each state has an equal voice, with two senators elected from each to make 100 members in all. In the House, the states have locally elected representatives in proportion to their population (revised at each decennial census), the total number being 435.

Members of the House of Representatives are elected to a two-year term, and senators for six years. Congressmen are aided by a personal staff, which might number seven to ten for a representative and fifteen to thirty for a senator. Each house of Congress meets in its own chamber in the Capitol Building in Washington DC. In January of each odd-numbered year a new Congress is said to begin; the one starting in January 1973 is the 92nd Congress since the first one convened in 1789. The House is presided over by a Speaker, who is not an impartial chairman but a party politician who can descend from his chair to participate in the debate. The President of the Senate (the Vice-President) can vote, but only in the event of a tie. Both houses of Congress are supposed to have an equal say in the affairs of state. Important figures in each house are the 'majority' (Democratic) and 'minority' (Republican) leaders, who lead the debates and bring forward the party programmes. There are also 'whips', who keep track of legislation and of the votes of their party Congressmen.

New legislation starts with the introduction of a bill by a member of Congress. It is then referred to one of the standing or select committees, to which the members have delegated much of their responsibilities. About nine-tenths of the legislative business of Congress is done in the committees, the reliance on this system having come in the nineteenth century to save time on the house floors. There are over 300 committees and sub-committees, and they can meet in public or in private. The committee system has assumed very great importance in American government, and power in both houses of Congress is now wielded not so much by the individual members as by a handful of the principal committee chairmen, who are nationally known political figures.

Representation on the committees tends to reflect party strength in the Senate and the House. The chairmen are selected according to the 'seniority rule', and are the longest-serving members of the majority party. There has been a movement recently to abolish the seniority system, which rewards age rather than ability and greatly enhances the authority of the chairman and the senior or 'ranking' members.

The committee system has no constitutional authority but relies simply on tradition, and it dominates the activities of both houses. The chairmen are not responsible to Congress, despite the power which they have over legislation. But they are directly responsible to the states and the districts which elected them, and this means that regional and local interests can easily take precedence over national interests in the minds and actions of the chairmen.

Each committee has members with experience or special interests in the area of its concern. But the committees also have members whose role is to defend their local interests or those of some part of the business world or military establishment. Some Congressmen with experience in a particular field have been denied membership on the relevant committee, because their views might have conflicted with those of the members supporting sectional interests.

The standing committees and their chairmen can delay legislation for years if they do not like it, simply by preventing it from reaching the Senate or the House. When it gets out of committee, it can be further delayed by a 'filibuster', which takes the form of senators making long speeches or using up time by strict adherence to the rules of the Senate or House. Bills may be amended on the floor of Congress, and their content is subject to all manner of public and private negotiations. When they finally reach the desk of the President he may veto them, but this can be overturned in Congress by a two-thirds majority. The legislative process, described here in briefest outline only, may sound extremely complex and time-consuming, but it does allow a very full consideration of the measures proposed.

Despite the powers vested in it by Constitution, Congress itself now rarely initiates important legislation. Its main function is to process the programme of the President. It can delay and modify legislation very considerably, and has the important additional power of being able to withhold the funds needed to finance programmes. Thus the checks and balances still apply.

Special interests and pressure groups exert considerable influence on the Congress. Much of the contact between the representatives of these groups and the members of Congress is informal and conducted in the lobbies, hence the term 'lobby-ing'. Among the most powerful lobbies are those representing agriculture, labour, various branches of industry, the veterans, the military, the medical profession, and people who like guns. In some cases their influence on major legislation has been critical, as for example in the expensive campaign of the American Medical Association in opposition to financial assist-ance towards medical care for the aged, and the opposition of the National Rifle Association to legislation for the licensing of sporting guns. Clearly, lobbying does not reflect the interests of all the people, and is a major factor in the distortion of the democratic process. Many organisations employ permanent professional lobbyists in Washington. In other cases an elected representative may see his role as that of the servant of some special business interest (with which he may be personally associated) rather than of the people of his district.

THE JUDICIAL BRANCH

The Judicial branch of federal government is headed by the Supreme Court. This consists of a Chief Justice and eight Asso-ciate Justices, who meet in the Supreme Court Building in Washington DC, and determine the constitutionality of issues brought before them. It is sometimes observed that the Con-stitution means what these judges at any one time say it means. As custodians and interpreters of the Constitution, the members of the Supreme Court occupy a very important position in the complex and interdependent system of American government.

The Supreme Court can declare unconstitutional an act of Congress, or right a wrong against an individual. It can pass judgement on state and local government legislation, and con-sider appeals against the decisions of lower courts when there is a likelihood that constitutional rights are involved. In an aver-age term from October to June the Supreme Court considers perhaps 15,000 cases. The majority are disposed of by the brief decision that the subject matter is either not proper or not of sufficient importance to warrant court review. Only 250 to 300 cases are decided on their merits, and about half these are announced in full published opinions written by the judges. The decisions are made by a majority vote, and judges may write dissenting opinions if they disagree with the majority.

The Constitution does not state any qualifications for Supreme Court judges. Previous experience on the bench is usual but not essential, and members have come from different backgrounds. As appointments to the court are made by the President, they can be a gift for services rendered, but on the whole this form of political patronage has been dispensed with great care. The requirement that the Senate confirm the President's nominees provides a check on the abuse of the power of the chief executive in this area. Nevertheless, a President who is able to make a number of appointments to the Supreme Court during his term of office can influence the nature of the court for many years to come. Once on the court, judges can remain there until death, and a term of two decades is not unusual.

The Supreme Court stands at the apex of the federal and state judicial systems. Below it are the District Courts—trial courts with general federal jurisdiction, of which there is at least one in every state. There are also Courts of Appeal, created to relieve the Supreme Court of considering all appeals in cases originally decided by the federal trial courts.

PARTY POLITICS AND ELECTIONS

The United States has essentially a two-party system, though third parties have flourished at times. The major parties are the Democrats and the Republicans. Although the Democrats tend towards the liberal position and the Republicans towards the conservative, both parties reflect within their ranks almost every shade of opinion except the radical or Socialist left. There is a substantial overlap at the centre, and right-wing (usually southern) Democrats are often far more conservative than some Republicans, while the more liberal of both parties look very much the same. In fact, to try to interpret American party politics on a conventional 'left' to 'right' continuum is impracticable.

Neither party has a very clear and distinctive ideology. Generally, the Republicans are the party of business, the rich, the middle classes who have 'made it' in the competitive economic world, the older Protestant stock of the north (the WASPs), and those with conservative views. The Democrats are traditionally the party of organised labour, the ethnic groups in the cities (they were originally the party of the immigrants), the Blacks and other racial minorities, the intellectuals, and the middle-class liberals.

The absence of a non-Communist left, such as the Labour Party in Britain, is an important feature of American politics. Fear and hatred of Communism still pervades American society, and left-wing groups have traditionally been harassed, alienated, and driven to extreme positions, almost as though by design there is no place for them. In fact, 'Socialist' is a term of denigration somewhat milder than 'Communist', frequently invoked to describe anything to the left of one's own political views. Some left-wing groups talk optimistically of a student-worker coalition of the kind which has brought revolutionary change to certain other countries, but in the United States today such a proposition seems quite untenable. The blue-collar workers are in general satisfied with the status quo and the high material living standards it offers, and their patriotic zeal is in sharp conflict with the anti-establishment activists of the university campuses. The workers seem more likely to embrace extremist movements on the right, as is shown by their affiliation with the Ku-Klux-Klan, the John Birch Society, and the American Independence Party of George Wallace.

At the beginning of the 1970s the American Independence Party was the only third party with any pretension to national status. Wallace took over 10 per cent of the vote in 1968, compared with 43·4 per cent for Nixon (Republican) and 42·7 per cent for Humphrey (Democrat). Wallace's support was then largely in the South, and his candidacy was in the southern tradition of 'states' rights', the main theme of which is suspicion of the power of federal government and a reluctance to abandon racial segregation. The widening support for Wallace during the early stages of the 1972 Presidential campaign, particularly in some of the northern industrial states, seems part of a contemporary realignment of party political affiliations which is significantly changing the traditional coalitions.

Political organisation starts locally at the 'precinct' level. There are roughly 170,000 precincts in the country, with an average of about 650 potential voters. The party precinct leader or 'captain' has the job of getting the vote out on election day, and this he achieves with a combination of persuasion and the distribution of favours. Above the precincts come the party county committees, and then the state committees. It is through this complex organisational pyramid that candidates for elected office are supposed to make their way, satisfying the local party officials, the special interests groups, and on occasions their constituents, as to their loyalty and dedication.

During the nineteenth century the ease with which a few powerful individuals could control the party nominations for elected office led to the introduction of 'primary' elections. Now most of the states use primaries to select the party candidates for Congress. In states or districts where one party is dominant, the primaries in effect elect the Congressman, because once over this hurdle he will face only token opposition in the actual election. The Presidential primaries are particularly important, as they provide prospective candidates for party nomination to run for President with the opportunity to test their strength in different parts of the country. An impressive showing in the state primaries is usually necessary if a candidate is to be considered seriously at the national party convention which meets to select the Presidential nominee; the McGovern campaign for the Democratic nomination in 1972 is a good illustration. The Presidential primaries start about eight months before the general Presidential election, and prospective candidates may have made their aspirations known up to a year before the primaries. Election campaigns in the United States can be long and arduous, especially for the Presidency.

The national party conventions at which the Presidential and Vice-Presidential 'ticket' is selected are elaborate ritualistic events, almost incomprehensible to outsiders. The party in each state sends delegates, to first elect the Presidential nominee and then (usually) to confirm the running mate of his choosing. Speeches of nomination are made, interspersed by carefully planned demonstrations of support accompanied by banners, bands, and much general merriment. In huddled groups on the floor, and in the legendary smoke-filled rooms of the hotels, representatives of the leading candidates will bargain or 'wheel and deal' for delegate support. The states are called in alphabetical order to place or second nominations, and to have their delegates vote. The process is repeated, if necessary, with further frantic back-stage manoeuvring, until one candidate achieves the required majority. He then becomes the nominee of his party. Much incidental social activity accompanies the politics.

The general election takes place in the November following the conventions. Along with the Presidential election, there will be the election of Congressmen and also the multiplicity of local officials. Some people will vote a 'straight' Democratic or Republican ticket, while others will 'split' their ticket—perhaps voting for the Democratic national candidates and the

------

Richard Nixon at a Republican Party gathering, showing the carnival quality of American political campaigning.

Three Southern politicians, representing a broad spectrum of the past, present and future political leadership.

Republicans locally. If the national candidates of one party are very successful, for example if there is a 'landslide' vote for one of the two Presidential and Vice-Presidential tickets, the number of people who vote the straight party line will mean that many local candidates are swept to victory 'on the coat-tails' of the national candidates.

The Presidential election is conducted by the Electoral College. This means that in the general election people vote for a state 'slate' of delegates rather than for the President himself, the slate being pledged to support the candidate with most votes in that state. States have Electoral College representation in accordance with their number of congressmen, so it broadly reflects population. Thus it is particularly important for a Presidential candidate to carry the bigger states, such as New York, Illinois and California. Under the Electoral College system it is quite possible for the candidate with the minority of the popular vote to be elected, by carrying the critical states.

Not everyone can run for the Presidency. The Constitution requires that the candidate be at least thirty-five years old, and a natural-born citizen with at least fourteen years' residence. It is also expected that *he* (not she) will be white, and with a conventional private life. To be female, black or divorced could be

---

Inside a modern oil refinery—advanced industrial technology shown in the computerised control room of the distillation plant, at a Standard Oil facility.

Building a lobster boat in Maine—still some room for the 'little man' in the American economy, despite the general dominance of 'big business'.

D

a much more serious drawback than questions of personal ability, vision or integrity. By virtue of reaching the position of candidacy with reasonable prospects of victory, he will also have satisfied the rigorous process of party scrutiny, and attracted sufficient financial backing to support the very high expenses of a national election campaign. The growing cost of electioneering in the United States creates an insurmountable barrier for all but a small minority; Richard Nixon's 1972 campaign is estimated to have cost over $35 million.

STATE AND LOCAL GOVERNMENT

Each state possesses all the machinery of independent government. It has its own executive branch under an elected Governor, its own legislature with its two chambers (except in Nebraska where there is only one), and its own judicial system with a supreme or superior court. In short, each state has a system closely mirroring the national system of government.

Each state also has its own constitution. It has powers of taxation, and state departments to administer education, regulate commerce, and perform the many other functions of a major unit of government. The annual budget of some of the states, such as California and New York, is comparable with that of large European countries. Within their boundaries the powers of state government are considerable, although their autonomy is subject to federal checks. The constitutional relationship between nation and state is such that misgovernment on the part of a state is not a matter for federal concern, unless federal authority is infringed—for example, in the area of citizen rights protected by the national Constitution. Thus the federal government can force states to comply with rulings of the Supreme Court, as in school desegregation and other civil rights areas where some southern states attempted to defy the Court.

The states are proud of their independence. Each one has a state capitol building in its seat of government, and symbols of identity such as its flag, its flower, its bird, its nickname, and its motto, which is reproduced on automobile license plates (thus Florida is 'The Sunshine State', Illinois 'Land of Lincoln', and so on). The quality of state government and the resources to support it can vary considerably, and this leads to differences in the quality and extent of state services. Some states have highly innovating programmes; others have legislatures largely sold out to powerful business interests, and subject to all manner of dubious practices.

Within the states there is a system of local government with smaller administrative units. There are over 3,000 counties, and within them large numbers of cities and other urban places with some degree of administrative autonomy. There are almost 25,000 school systems operating within the country, and over 43,000 separate police forces. The end result is further lack of uniformity of services across the country. Rather than risk federal 'interference' in local affairs, the American people seem generally to accept these differences, believing that local government is more democratic and responsive to the people than are anonymous Washington bureaucrats.

An important feature of American local politics is the number of officials who are elected by the people, rather than appointed on the basis of experience, special skills, or merit. For example, at the time of the national Presidential election various state congressional seats and state offices will be filled, and also such posts as state university trustees, county clerks, state's attorneys, coroners and commissioners. Such local posts as judge and school-board member are also determined by the processes of American democracy.

Somewhat independent of state and county government, though often tied into the same web of party politics, is the government of the cities. There are three main types of city government: the mayor and council, the city commission, and the city manager. The mayor and council is the oldest, and still the most common in the big cities where the mayor as chief executive can exert very considerable power. Mayors of the largest cities can gain national political stature, as has been the case with Daley of Chicago and Lindsay of New York. The city commission system, introduced at the beginning of the present century, makes the mayor more of a figurehead president of a body which performs both legislative and executive functions. Under the city manager system the people's elected representatives appoint a professional to manage and oversee the affairs of the city, a measure that is supposed to have the advantage of eliminating corruption and petty politics in the running of the city.

NATIONAL SECURITY AND DEFENCE

National security and defence assume particular significance in the United States, in view of its role conventionally described as 'defender of the free world'. Internal security is also of vital interest to the American people, many of whom still fear some kind of Communist take-over from within. Added to this is the increasing lawlessness of society, as expressed in rising crime rates, and the growing militancy of some deprived and minority groups who talk openly of revolution as the only way of re-ordering national priorities and creating their conception of a just society.

In the international arena the outposts of national defence comprise a ring of military bases and warning systems which partially surround Russia and China. Closely connected with these are major multilateral military alliances, chiefly the North Atlantic Treaty Organisation (NATO, 1949), the Organisation of American States (OAS, 1948), and the South-East Asia Treaty Organisation (SEATO, 1954). Overall responsibility for foreign affairs, including the signing of treaties and the maintenance of friendly relations with other countries, is vested in the Department of State. The Foreign Service, responsible to the Department of State, comprises the ambassadors, consular officials and so on, who represent American interests overseas.

Major decisions relating to national security are the responsibility of the President. To advise him there is the National

Security Council, made up of top representatives of military, defence and intelligence agencies. However, in recent years the President appears to have relied increasingly on one major personal adviser on matters of global political and military strategy.

Implementing national defence (or offence) policy requires military forces. Until 1947 the Army, Navy and Air Force were independent, and answered only to the President as Commander-in-Chief. Then the National Military Establishment was set up, to provide for the co-ordination of the three forces under a civilian Secretary of Defense. The Selective Service System is responsible for inducting into the armed forces persons required in addition to those who enter as volunteers. The total number of military personnel on active duty in 1970 was 2,874,000, to which must be added 1,152,000 civilians employed by military agencies. The total payroll of all these persons was about $30 billion, and the national defence budget as a whole amounted to about $80 billion of the $215 billion or so total federal outlays for all purposes. Soldiers who have fought in foreign wars have a rather special status in the United States, and certain privileges, and these are taken care of by the Veterans Administration.

A successful national defence strategy is dependent on a steady supply of accurate information. The Central Intelligence Agency, responsible to the President, has the job of bringing together intelligence and making recommendations to the National Security Council. Exactly how far the CIA spy network extends is, of course, unknown, as it acts with great secrecy. Its budget is not published, and Congress has only a very vague idea of what it is doing. There is probably some truth in the suggestions made in recent years that the CIA is not averse to influencing the internal affairs of foreign nations if it judges this to be in the national interest. There is some current concern that the agency may not be subject to sufficient control, in the sensitive area where foreign policy, economic aid and the gathering of intelligence overlap.

The US Information Agency explains United States policy to other nations. It is the overseas propaganda arm of the

Executive branch, and attempts to convey national policy and the American way of life in the most favourable light.

The maintenance of internal security, and law and order on a national scale, is the function of the Federal Bureau of Investigation. Responsible to the Department of Justice, the FBI has as its major duty the investigation of violations of federal laws relating to such matters as espionage, sabotage, treason, and the transportation of stolen goods over state lines. Under the long leadership of J. Edgar Hoover, the FBI was able to develop a large measure of autonomy, and co-operation with the Attorney-General has not always been complete. There is also a Secret Service, responsible to the Department of the Treasury, and with the duty of protecting the President and his family and the Vice-President, as well as detecting forgery and currency crimes. If there is a threat to internal peace, order and safety, the National Guard can be used to protect life and property; in peacetime this force is under the command of the state Governors.

Just as the extent of the overseas spy network is unknown, it is difficult to establish just how far personal surveillance for security reasons extends within the United States. The armed forces and the FBI have certainly been keeping files on the activities of groups ranging from Black militants to peace advocates, and at times appear to have an unusual perception of the kind of people who may threaten national security. Undoubtedly some of this activity has been political and directed towards outspoken opponents of the interests of the military/business establishment rather than at real or potential criminals. What internal security measures are appropriate in a free society is a matter not easily resolved in contemporary America.

THE NATURE OF AMERICAN POLITICS

There are some important differences between American government and the system in Great Britain where so many American institutions originated. One of the most obvious is the general lack of a professional non-political civil service or corps of local government officers, which serve succeeding administrations without change in personnel. Another is the conspicuous secret service and the elaborate security precautions necessary to protect the President, and also his family, advisers, and members of Congress. Another difference is that neither of the major political parties is staffed by representatives of the labour unions; attempts to produce political parties based on social class have been unsuccessful in the United States, though there is some tendency towards class alignment. But the most conspicuous difference is probably the existence of the patronage system and what is colloquially known as 'graft'.

Some of the difficulties in American government, both nationally and locally, can obviously be attributed to the power of human greed. Business has traditionally had things very much its own way, operating with a minimum of governmental restraints, and in the past almost any course of action has been countenanced in the pursuit of economic gain. But the Americans value their vote, whether it be for President or town dog-catcher, and no one can gain power by denying them this sacred right of choice. Those who wish to influence or co-opt the governmental decision-making process for their own ends have thus had to devise ways of achieving this through the electoral process, by controlling the party machines which put up the candidates and by seeing that those who co-operate get their reward.

The United States is a land of powerful conflicting interests, which the political process has somehow to reconcile. The history of American politics is often portrayed as a perpetual search for the consensus which best represents the diverse interests and aspirations of its varied peoples and pressure groups. Politics are thus a practical matter for pragmatic men of the world rather than a field for scholars engaged in deep philosophical debate, and ideology generally has to concede to realism as the necessary compromise is sought. The fortunes of the individual citizen in such a system are closely related to his capacity to influence the decision-making process, as part of a power bloc with enough potential votes or financial resources to promote its own interests effectively in competition with others. The challenge to the politician is to appeal simultaneously to a broad spectrum of a heterogeneous population, powerful elements in which may be making mutually exclusive demands.

The defeat of George McGovern in the 1972 presidential election illustrated the consequences of a failure to gain such a broad base of support. With a platform of less aggressive foreign policy and greater spending on domestic programmes such as social welfare, the Republicans were able to portray him as unduly radical. He thus lost the support of some of the traditional sources of Democratic strength, including organised labour, and failed to command the centre of the political spectrum where elections are won or lost. Many voters split their tickets, to give Richard Nixon almost 60 per cent of the popular vote in a 'landslide' victory, but denying him the control of Congress needed to facilitate the passage of his legislative programme. The paradox of millions of the working class preferring a conservative, business-oriented candidate to one resembling a European social democrat is partly explained by the ease with which the Americans can still be persuaded to reject anything which might be considered left-wing policies. It is also being interpreted as an outcome of the desire for a period of calm following the turbulent 1960s with their 'new society' programmes, civil rights legislation, peace marches and student demonstrations. It seems a classic case of choosing the devil they know to the one they don't.

As Richard Nixon's second term of office gets under way, the prospect at home is of more conservative domestic policies on such matters as welfare and civil liberties, with the emphasis on efficient management, saving money and reducing the role of the federal government in state and local affairs. In the foreign policy arena it is likely to be a continuation of the existing combination of high level diplomacy and the aggressive pursuit of national self-interest, backed up by demonstrated military might.

3

How the Economy Works

PRESIDENT Calvin Coolidge once said, 'The chief business of America is business.' There are almost 12 million businesses in the United States, including farms, manufacturing establishments and services, and the making and spending of money are major national preoccupations. The combination of rich resources and an energetic people has helped to create the greatest economy in the world, and the most prosperous nation in the history of mankind.

The United States produces about one-third of all the world's manufactured goods, and an even greater share of its services. It uses over one-third of all the world's energy. Americans drive 56 per cent of the world's passenger cars and 40 per cent of its commercial vehicles. They use half the world's telephones, almost half its radios and two-fifths of its television sets. The Gross National Product has recently passed the landmark of $1,000 billion a year, and this is expected to have risen by a further $500 billion by 1980. Per capita GNP is about $4,500, or almost $1,000 more than in Sweden, the nearest rival. The growth of the American economy in recent years has been sufficient to sustain not only a high level of domestic prosperity but also $150 billion in foreign aid since 1945.

Yet the American economy cannot be portrayed entirely by the conventional statistics and superlatives. Despite the high material living standards of most of the people, the nation cannot provide an adequate income, full social services, and a decent environment for a substantial minority of the population. The way the economy works is a matter of growing public

61

concern and of increasing governmental intervention and regulation.

The United States is usually characterised as having a free-enterprise or free-market economy. In theory, such a system works roughly as follows: the individual takes the initiative in going into business to produce goods or services to satisfy an observed demand, and if successful his enterprise and capital investment are rewarded in the form of profits; consumers make choices between the alternative ways of spending or saving their incomes, prices being determined in the market by the forces of supply and demand; competition between producers leads to the survival of only the most efficient and innovative, and prevents inflated prices and profits; the end result is an allocation of scarce resources between alternative uses or productive activities in a way which reflects the collective wishes of the people as expressed by their market-place choices. The profit motive is the essential driving force, ensuring that products and techniques are steadily improved by rewarding businesses and their investors according to the risks they take and the popularity of their goods or services.

As a system which emphasises individual initiative, freedom of choice, and recompense for work, the market economy seems especially suited to the values and temperament of the American people. It embodies the heroic figure of the man who pulls himself up by his own bootstraps against great adversity, to build up a successful business. The implied faith that the outcome of everyone pursuing his own economic self-interest will reflect the collective will of the people is also appealing in a democracy.

Economic reality seldom accords accurately with theory, however. The process described above may have existed to a large extent in earlier stages of economic development, and there are certainly elements of it today. But the free-market economy described in elementary textbooks, Rotary Club speeches, and government leaflets extolling the virtues of capitalism is at best a considerable over-simplification of what actually takes place. For example, despite the lip service paid to competition, a normal business objective is to eliminate competitors as far as government regulation permits, in order to raise prices and increase profits. The power of certain major corporations and labour unions is such that prices and wages are often fixed without much recourse to the market-place, and consumer demand can be manipulated effectively by advertising. The influence of the federal government, as regulator and as an important customer for privately produced goods and services, is such as to lead some economists to suggest that America may now have as much of a planned economy as a free-market system. With the range of different interpretations which professional economists place on the present state of the national economy it is difficult to be conclusive here; all that can be offered are some facts concerning the organisation, ownership and control of the production process.

The basic unit of production is the individual business. There are three types in the United States—sole proprietorships owned by a single person, partnerships owned by two or more persons, and corporations owned by stockholders. Proprietorships are by far the most numerous, accounting for four out of five of all businesses. But the corporations do the bulk of the business, with about nine-tenths of all receipts.

Holding stock in corporations is a way in which many people who are not proprietors or partners participate in business and share its profits. According to the New York Stock Exchange, there were over 30 million stockholders in 1970 and one in four American adults now hold stock compared with one in sixteen twenty years ago. Two-thirds are in the $5,000–15,000 annual income range, so shareholding is certainly not the exclusive province of the rich. One of the main features of the American economy is the way in which people are eager to participate directly in business, either as shareholders or on their own account.

Increased stockholding in recent years has brought about a

diffusion of corporate ownership and control. During earlier
stages of national economic development the big American
business was typically run by a single individual, usually the
founder, who was often exclusively devoted to making as much
money as possible in the short run. At the extreme he became
the 'robber baron', raping the earth, exploiting his workers, and
bribing legislators and officials. This type of businessman has
now been largely replaced by the professional salaried manager,
usually with little or no stockholding in the corporation, and
more concerned with rational long-term planning and with the
security of the enterprise than with maximising short-term
profits. These are the 'organisation men' described by William H.
Whyte and the 'technostructure' of John Kenneth Galbraith.
This has been accompanied by a growing anonymity of business, as the great conglomerates and financial houses obscure
some of their holdings by the use of nominees or 'front
names'.

Though numerically America is a land of small businesses—
farms, service stations, restaurants, and 'Ma and Pa' establishments—it is not here that the productive capacity and output
is concentrated. Half of all businesses take less than $10,000 a
year, but these account for only 1 per cent of total business
receipts, while those with takings of over $500,000 a year (only
3 per cent of all businesses), account for almost four-fifths of
total receipts. Less than 2 per cent of total assets are in the 60
per cent of corporations with under $100,000 assets, while the
one in a thousand corporations with assets over $250 million
control over half of all the assets. The concentration is increasing: in 1948 the hundred largest corporations had about 40 per
cent of all assets, but now it is almost 50 per cent.

Size brings efficiency through economies of scale, and has
been a major factor in making a wide range of consumer goods
available to the American people at a price they can afford. But
a few industries are now dominated to such an extent by one
giant corporation that some of the advantages of the competitive system are lost. IBM controls 70 per cent of computer
business, General Motors half the automobile market, and US

Steel, Dupont and Alcoa have only three or four healthy competitors in their respective industries. Such corporations can often fix their prices fairly freely. Extreme forms of monopoly are subject to legal restraint, however, and the customer ultimately has the freedom not to buy a product unless he sees it as a necessity.

Whereas in classical economic theory industry responds to an expressed demand from consumers for a particular product or service, it is becoming increasingly the case that such demand is created or stimulated by business itself through advertising. Such demands are sometimes termed 'wants' rather than 'needs'. Total national expenditures on advertising doubled in the 1950s and again in the 1960s, to reach about $20 billion today. Television advertising is now particularly important, with great skill exercised in associating products like automobiles and mouth washes with masculinity or sex appeal, and playing on the conformist nature of the American people. Since the end of the 1940s the proportion of the family budget available for other purchases after the required expenditure on food has gone up from three-fifths to four-fifths, and a growing surplus of spending power has thus been created. The capacity of business to influence consumer behaviour, through powerful mass-media advertising, may help to explain the relatively large amount of money spent in the United States on consumer goods compared with social services.

Another area in which big business exercises considerable influence over the national allocation of resources is in the defence and aero-space industries. That national defence and the production of the associated weapons are a huge business in contemporary America can be judged from the fact that the total value of shipments from defence-oriented industries is about $150 billion annually, and their employment almost 5 million persons. The value of the defence contracts awarded in 1970 alone was over £33 billion. The research and development costs involved in a new missile system or military aircraft are enormous, and the defence contractors have to work very closely with the Defense Department. As early as the 1950s President

Eisenhower warned against the emergence of a 'military-industrial complex', and there is much current concern that the collusion between the Defense Department and their contractors necessitated by the complex process of arming a modern military power may be having undesirable results. There have been some notorious cases of 'cost overruns' in weapons manufacturing, with the final product costing much more than the original contract figure, and there is a growing feeling that many billions of dollars have been wasted in recent years on inefficient or unnecessary new weapons.

The position of the federal government as the customer of the major defence and aero-space industries has had the effect of bringing government into the business system to an extent previously unknown. It is now held that the commercial failure of a vital defence contracting firm can be contrary to the national security interest, as was the case when the Lockheed Corporation got into financial difficulties and had to be kept alive by a very large government-supported loan. This has led some people to propose the nationalisation of the areo industry, and of other industries heavily dependent on national defence policy for their prosperity. It is also argued that public ownership might be in order for the coal-mining industry, which is notorious for its disdain for the earth from which it extracts its wealth and for the health and safety of its employees.

Nationalisation is, of course, anathema to the business community and to the vast majority of the American populace. It would be interpreted as 'creeping Socialism'—the worst of all possible ills, and a threat to the great free-enterprise system. Direct government participation in economic activity in the United States, at both the national and local level, is confined to the provision of public services, and incursion into the private sector would be considered highly improper. Yet in some ways the Americans already have a planned economy. Galbraith argues, in *The New Industrial State*, that the federal government and the major corporations plan their joint and independent economic activity to a very great extent, and that this planning is required by the complex nature of the modern economy.

One of the interesting ironies of the contemporary economic scene is that some of the strongest supporters of the principles of free enterprise and competition are themselves the receivers of large government subsidies. An example is the oil depletion allowance, which provides a large tax reduction for an industry which does not appear to suffer from any great financial difficulties. Another is the system of agricultural price supports, through which some by no means impoverished farmers get subsidies. The relatively small welfare payments and the inadequate social services available to the less fortunate citizens have led to charges that the American economic system is one of rugged individualism for the poor and socialism for the rich.

Whatever the inequities of the distribution of wealth, the American economic system has performed very successfully in recent years, by the criterion of the material well-being of the majority of the population. However, increasing public awareness of the less fortunate social and environmental consequences of rapid and largely unregulated economic growth is likely to bring increasing government intervention. The President has a Council of Economic Advisers, who can recommend to him appropriate economic, financial and fiscal measures, and he can exercise considerable control of the economy through executive order. Whatever the views of the die-hard advocates of free enterprise, the American economy seems destined to be more centrally planned in the future than it has ever been.

PRODUCTION AND INCOME

Over 80 million Americans are employed in some civilian productive process. Almost 40 million are white-collar workers —professional people, technicians, managers, officials, proprietors, clerical workers and salesworkers. More than 26 million are blue-collar workers—craftsmen, foremen, operatives and non-farm labourers. Over 10 million are in services, both household and business, and just over 3 million are farm workers. The composition of the workforce has changed considerably since the beginning of the century, when blue-collar workers outnumbered white-collar workers two to one. Employment in white-collar and service occupations has increased sevenfold, while blue-collar employment has risen much less rapidly and agricultural employment has dropped sharply. At present there are about 5 million unemployed, slightly under 6 per cent of all the civilian labour force and almost 10 per cent of non-whites.

In 1970 the Gross National Product, or the total national output of goods and services at market prices, amounted to $976.5 billion. About 84 billion are accounted for by capital consumption allowances and 92 billion by business taxes and other liabilities, to leave a National Income of 800 billion—almost identical to the figure for all personal income. Personal tax and other non-tax payments reduce this to a disposable personal income of 685 billion, of which 50 billion are saved and the rest spent.

The National Income in 1970 originated as follows:

Industry	$ billion	% of total
Agriculture, forestry and fisheries	24.6	3.1
Mining and construction	49.5	6.2
Manufacturing	221.0	27.6
Transportation	30.3	3.8
Communication and utilities	31.0	3.9
Wholesale and retail trade	121.8	15.2
Finance, insurance and real estate	88.5	11.1
Services	104.4	13.0
Government and governmental enterprise	125.2	15.6
From other nations	4.5	0.5
Total National Income	800.8	100.0

Compared with twenty years ago, the proportional contribution of agriculture and so on has more than halved, transportation has almost halved, and manufacturing and mining have been reduced by about 10 per cent. The contribution of wholesale and retail trade has also gone down slightly, but there have been substantial increases in the proportion coming from finance, etc, and other services, and the government contribution has gone up by over 50 per cent.

Manufacturing still contributes more than a quarter of national income. The leading durable goods industries, measured by their contributions to national income, are transportation equipment including automobiles ($34 billion), machinery ($25 billion) and electrical machinery ($21 billion), followed by primary metal industries, fabricated metal industries, stone, clay and glass products, instruments, lumber and wood products, and furniture and fixtures. The leading nondurable goods industries are food and kindred products ($19 billion), chemicals and allied products ($16 billion), and textiles and clothing ($16 billion), followed by printing and publishing, paper, petroleum refining, rubber and plastics, and leather goods. Manufacturing is heavily concentrated in the 'major manufacturing belt' extending roughly from Boston to Chicago, with the Middle Atlantic and North East Central Regions accounting for half the total employment and value added. The South Atlantic Region and the Pacific each contribute a further 12 per cent (approximately) of national manufacturing.

In services, the leading sectors are medical and other health services, and miscellaneous business services. Under finance, etc, the real-estate business is the major activity. In wholesale and retail, retail is the more important income contributor by a ratio of about seven to four. In agriculture, the most important crops by value are corn (maize), hay, cotton, soybeans, fruit and wheat. The value of farm production is roughly equally divided between livestock, livestock products (including poultry) and dairying on the one hand, and field and tree crops together with vegetables and horticulture on the other.

The American economy generates the incomes of the most prosperous workers in the world. Average earnings in 1970 in various sectors were as follows:

E

Industry	Average hourly $ earnings
Mining	3.84
Construction	5.22
Manufacturing durable goods	3.56
Manufacturing non-durable goods	3.08
Transportation, communication and utilities	3.85
Wholesale and retail trade	2.71
Finance, insurance and real estate	3.07
Services	2.84
Average for all private sector	3.23

There are, however, individual occupations which pay considerably less than these wage levels; for example employees in catering establishments average only $1.85 an hour, many agricultural workers get less than this (their average daily earnings in 1969 were only about $8.50), and in some cities the (black) domestic helps are lucky if they get more than $1.00 an hour. Some of the highest earnings are in construction: 1971 rates for electricians were $7.95 an hour, for plumbers $8.50, bricklayers $7.83, and carpenters $7.62. Earnings are also subject to regional variations; for example the average hourly pay of manufacturing workers range from $2.43 in Mississippi to $4.15 in Michigan, and rise to $4.66 in Alaska.

Some average annual salaries in selected occupations are listed below, rounded to the nearest hundred dollars (figures for 1970):

Occupation	Average salary ($)
Attorney	33,000
Chemist	27,700
Engineer	25,400
Personnel director	21,900
Accountant	15,500
Auditor	14,000
Buyer	13,900
Engineering technician	11,000

Draftsman	10,000
Secretary	8,100
Accounting clerk	6,800
File clerk or Typist	5,500

In each case these rates refer to top grade employees, as identified in a Department of Labour survey, and salaries of beginners might be half the figure shown. In public service, rates of remuneration are roughly comparable to the above for a given level of skill or expertise, though the opportunities for extremely high salaries are less. The highest earnings in America are made in private business, and in the legal and medical professions.

The median income of the white American family is now just over $10,000 a year. For non-Whites it is about $6,500. Half of all white families get more than $10,000 a year, one in five gets over $15,000, and only one in six gets less than $5,000. For non-Whites only one family in four gets over $10,000, and more than half get less than $7,000. These income levels are high compared with other countries, but an American family of four living in an urban area needs anything from $3,500 to $5,500 simply for bare necessities, and to live the full suburban middle-class way of life $10,000 would not be enough.

Almost 25 million Americans live below the official government poverty line, and in some southern states the proportion is at least one in five. A quarter of all persons over 65 years of age are classed as poor, as are one-third of all Blacks, but only one in ten of Whites and only about one in fifteen of Whites aged 22 to 64. At the other end of the wealth scale, the United States can boast 60,000 millionaires, and one in every hundred people has personal wealth of over $100,000. Despite the general spread of affluence in recent years, the distribution of income between rich and poor changes little; each group retains roughly the same share of national income as it did twenty years ago.

EXPENDITURE AND CONSUMPTION

The Americans are almost compulsive consumers and the stimulus to work provided by the need for more money to spend is a major driving force in the economic system. Nowhere in the world is there a greater range of goods and services to tempt the consumer, and probably nowhere else is there the same pressure to buy the material trappings and symbols of the affluent society.

There are two aspects of spending—public and private. Public spending is planned and allocated at the national level by the Federal Budget, the main items of which are as follows (1971 estimates):

Function	*$ billion*
National defence	76.4
International affairs and finance	3.6
Agricultural and rural development	5.3
Natural resources	2.6
Commerce and transportation	11.4
Community development and housing	2.9
Education and manpower	8.3
Health	14.3
Income security	55.5
Veterans' benefits and service	10.0
Interest	19.4
General government	4.4
Total outlays	212.8

(Note that because of rounding and certain transactions not included, the individual items will not add up to the total outlays.)

An important feature of the budget is the prominent place of defence expenditure, particularly compared with money spent on community development, health and education.

Total federal receipts in 1971 are estimated at $194 billion, which means a deficit of over $18 billion on outlays. The main sources of government income are about $90 billion from taxes on individual incomes, $30 billion from corporation earnings, and $50 billion from payroll taxes.

Public spending also takes place at the state and local level, and is allocated as follows: 36 per cent to education, 16 per cent to public welfare, hospitals and health, 12 per cent to highways, 7 per cent to utilities, etc, and the rest to other general expenditures. The money comes from a variety of sources: 24 per cent from property tax, 20 per cent from sales and gross receipts taxes, 15 per cent from the federal government, and 15 per cent from other taxes. The states vary considerably in the way they levy their taxes; most now tax personal incomes, but a few have not yet adopted a corporate profits tax. There is no general purchase tax, the nearest equivalent being the sales tax of generally 3 to 6 per cent levied on the sale of goods and some services and added to the price at the time of payment.

The allocation of personal spending is as follows, based on official figures for 1969:

Type of product	$ billion spent	$ of total
Food, beverages and alcohol	131.9	22.8
Clothing, accessories, and jewellery	59.4	10.3
Housing	84.0	14.5
Household operation, including equipment and utilities	81.5	14.1
Medical care	42.6	7.4
Personal business	31.9	5.5
Transportation	78.0	13.5
Recreation	36.3	6.3
Others	32.1	5.6
Total consumption	577.5	100.0

Department of Labour figures indicate that an average urban family of four spending about $11,500 on all goods and services in 1970 would have had the following outlays (in dollars): 2,800 on housing, 2,450 on food, 1,930 in personal taxes, 1,250 on transportation, 900 on clothing, 550 on medical care, 400 on recreation, 260 on personal care, and a further 820 on insurance, donations, education, and other costs.

Expenditures on personal consumption are now three times what they were twenty years ago, and there have been some changes in the way the money is allocated. The proportion spent on food products has gone down substantially, and there has also been a small reduction in spending on clothing and household operation. The largest proportional increase has been in medical expenses, rising from 4·6 per cent in 1950 to over 7·5 per cent in 1970. Housing, transportation and recreation also claim increasing proportions of personal expenditures. These changes reflect the affluent society, in which the material necessities of life assume a gradually smaller role in consumption.

In 1970, $60 billion was spent on imported goods and services. When other transactions are added, the total external payments come to $72.6 billion. This is offset by receipts from abroad amounting to $69.2 billion, including exports and income on US investments overseas. The difference between these two figures gives a balance of payments deficit of over $3.8 billion. The main commodities imported are machinery and transportation equipment including $4 billion worth of automobiles and motor cycles, other manufactured goods including metals, textiles and clothing, raw materials including petroleum and iron ore, and certain foodstuffs the most important of which is a billion dollars' worth of coffee. Most prominent in the exports from the United States are machinery and electrical goods (worth almost $12 billion), vehicles and aircraft, chemicals, and grain products. Also leaving the country are various types of foreign aid in the form of money, weapons, food and other commodities, and technical assistance.

BANKING, FINANCE AND INSURANCE

Banking exercises a critical role in the American economic system, both in arranging finance and in more direct participation in and control of the productive process. Banks come under the jurisdiction of both federal and state laws, the 'national' banks being supervised by the Comptroller of the Currency and state-chartered banks by officials of the states.

There are about 13,600 commercial banks in the United States. Their total assets are approximately $575 billion, half of which is accounted for by loans and discounts and a quarter by securities. Deposits are almost equally divided between demand and time accounts. As in the producing sector of the economy, banking is dominated by a few large concerns, and the concentration is increasing: about 48 per cent of all assets accrued to the largest fifty commercial banks in 1970, compared with 39 per cent in 1960.

Central banking functions are exercised by the Federal Reserve System, some of them being shared by the US Treasury. The system includes national banks, and such state banks as care to join. The Federal Deposit Insurance Corporation, set up in 1933, insures each bank depositor up to $20,000 in banks which are members of the Federal Reserve System or otherwise join the insurance fund. There were 4,000 bank suspensions in 1933 at the height of the depression (compared with only one in 1970), and the insurance system provides the small saver with some security against the losses from bank failures which were the unhappy experience of many Americans in the 1930s.

Government corporations and credit agencies can make credit available to specific groups of people, either by direct lending or by insuring or guaranteeing loans made by private lending institutions. The most important types of non-government credit agencies are savings and loan associations, insurance companies, finance companies, credit unions, and personal loan companies. The savings and loan associations, of which there are almost 6,000, are a particularly important source of mortgage loans.

Credit is extremely important to the American economic system, particularly as it facilitates consumer spending. Currency, including coin and paper money, represents only about one-fifth of the total media of exchange in the United States, with most payments being made by cheque. But in recent years the credit card has been assuming a rapidly increasing importance. About 1,400 banks now offer credit-card plans, compared with only 200 in 1967. A range of credit cards is part of the necessary contents of the middle-class purse or wallet; some can be used to purchase on credit almost any goods or service, whereas others can only be used at a certain department store or to fill the car with a certain brand of petrol. It is now much easier to shop and travel with a credit card than with a chequebook, because credit cards are generally issued only to people whose financial standing and past behaviour show them to be a good risk. To lose a good credit rating and hence the use of credit cards is something to be feared and avoided, because it can impose a serious brake on personal consumption. The availability of credit, like hire-purchase, has been an important part of the driving force of the American economy, both helping and encouraging people to buy things which they would not otherwise have considered.

In a land with so much in the way of material assets, insurance plays an important role in the economic system and in society at large. Although property, accident and health insurance are all big business, the major life insurance companies dominate the scene. While the number of commercial banks has been reduced slightly in the last twenty years through mergers, the number of life insurance companies has more than doubled. The major banks and insurance companies are very large investors in American business, and thus exercise considerable influence on the way the economic system operates.

SCIENCE AND TECHNOLOGY

A major contributory factor in the growth of the American economy is the massive application of science and technology to the improvement of products and processes. Years of laboratory and workshop testing, at a cost of millions of dollars, may precede the production and marketing of something new, whether an innovation in computer hardware or a toothpaste with a stripe in it. In 1971, almost $28 billion were spent in the United States on research and development. Slightly more than half of this money comes from the federal government, about two-fifths comes from private industry, and most of the rest is accounted for by universities and colleges.

There are over two and a half million scientists and technicians working in the United States. A major function of the education system, particularly higher education, is to train the required number of scientists and technicians to supply the rapidly growing needs for their services. The application of science and technology is selective. About two-thirds of all expenditures go on research and development in three areas: aircraft and missiles, electrical equipment and communications, and chemicals and allied products.

The space programme and the landing of men on the moon stands as the supreme expression of national technological prowess, and the expenditure involved show what the nation is prepared to do in support of such a demonstration. Between 1960 and 1972 the federal government spent about $65 billion on its space programme—enough to support its spending at current levels on health for five years and community development and housing for about fifteen years.

A few particular areas in science and technology which have had the greatest impact on American life and economy may be briefly mentioned. The first is power. American industry is highly mechanised and consumes enormous amounts of energy, added to which are the demands of domestic consumers with their gadgets to run and roomy houses to keep warm or cool. The country is rich in 'fossil fuels'—coal, oil and natural gas— but the inevitability of their eventual depletion has led to the development of other power sources, such as hydro-electricity and atomic energy.

Improvements in communication have also been very important. Scientific information from blueprints to cardiographs can now be transmitted instantaneously from one office or hospital to another. The almost universal adoption of television has given commercial advertisers access to the living rooms of most of the population. The telephone is a major means of conducting business and maintaining personal contact, and two-thirds of long-distance calls are now customer-dialled.

Developments in computer technology have been considerable, and no country in the world makes as much use of computers as the United States. They contribute to the general trend towards industrial automation, which has helped to improve labour productivity. They are used in offices, banks and elsewhere to run accounting and stock control systems. And they are used extensively in research to process numerical information in ways which would otherwise be impossible. But with technological advances and improved efficiency comes impersonality, and Americans find that in their daily lives they are increasingly dealing with machines rather than with people.

THE STATUS OF LABOUR

Compared with the contemporary situation in most other advanced industrial nations, the balance of power in the American economic system favours employer rather than employee. This is an inevitable outcome of the business orientation of American values, and of the inclination of most administrations and many elected officials to look after business interests first and the welfare of labour second. But far from having a low status, the average American worker probably feels that he is in an advantageous position, better paid than his counterparts elsewhere, with a better standard of living, with opportunities to 'make it' and build a business of his own if he has 'what it takes', and above all with the privilege of working in the greatest country in the world.

By and large American labour is not militant. Workers tend to see their interests as being closely coincident with those of management and the owners, and the blue-collar classes provide strong political support for the status quo. The leaders of labour, indistinguishable from management in their smart business suits, can frequently be heard upholding the virtues of competition and free enterprise, and in general seem barely touched by the thoughts of Marx, Mao, and other supposed heroes of the workers of the world. Only a minority of American workers belong to a union. At the beginning of the 1970s the figure was about 20 million, just over one in four of all non-agricultural employees and a slightly lower proportion than was the case ten years ago.

The reason for the relatively low unionisation of workers in America appears to be that organised labour has traditionally been viewed as a threat to business interests. The struggle for the rights of workers to organise, against the concerted opposition of employers and against courts which might regard combinations by workers as unlawful conspiracies, came very much later in the United States than, for example, in Britain. It is only since the great depression of the early 1930s that labour's right to bargain collectively has become almost universally recognised. More than a century of bitter and sometimes bloody conflict lies behind the present relatively secure position of organised labour. Even today there are many employers who will not permit their workers to join unions. Most union members belong to one of the 120 or so affiliates of the AFL-CIO (the American Federation of Labor and the Congress of Industrial Organizations).

As in other countries, the unions bargain with employers for improvement in wages or conditions of service. The strike is the last weapon of the unions, and in 1970 it was used about 6,000 times with each occurrence averaging 25 days. A well-known feature of labour relations in the United States is the Taft-Hartley Act of 1947, passed over the President's veto and against the bitter opposition of organised labour. This placed certain restrictions on union activities. Under one provision of the Act, strikers can be sent back to work for an eighty-day 'cooling off' period during which negotiations will proceed; it can be invoked in cases where a strike is judged to prejudice the national interest.

The unions do not have direct participation in the party political system as, for example, in the Labour Party in Britain. However, they are generally aligned with the Democrats, and a Democratic Presidential candidate would be expected to court the major unions for support.

There are various government programmes to assist people who are unemployed because of old age, disability, or lack of jobs. If someone loses his job through no fault of his own he can receive payments equal to roughly one-third of his wages through the Federal-State Unemployment Compensation. To get this he must register for work at a public employment exchange and report for possible jobs. About 50 million workers are covered, including most in industry.

CONSUMER AND ENVIRONMENTAL PROTECTION

Two important current concerns in the economy are the protection of consumers against inadequate goods and services and of the environment against pollution. These problems exist in all nations, but their recent emergence in the United States is of particular interest as a reflection of changing public awareness of the responsibilities of a modern industrial society.

American business prides itself on its ability to produce new and sophisticated goods and services. But its very success in doing this has created problems. There have been consumer movements in the past based on such issues as product safety and quality, deceptive practices, monopoly, aesthetics, and so on, but it is now being argued that the choice of goods has become so large and their technical complexity so great that the untrained individual cannot evaluate them. The consumer is thus becoming more and more powerless, in a market managed by the major corporations who have found that they can sell goods more successfully on the basis of design and styling than by their safety, health, durability, and so on. Business would counter this by arguing that the consumer can still exercise choice by not buying, and that the emphasis on styling and so on is a response to what he wants.

A particular problem is the 'built-in obsolescence' of many goods, a euphemism for the fact that they break down or become unfashionable after a relatively short time, thus necessitating their frequent repair or replacement. Intense competition has brought down the price of many consumer goods, but often at the expense of quality. The practice of periodic redesign of products, especially automobiles, means that last year's model is conspicuously out of date once the next model has appeared in the market-place. As a business strategy, the rapid obsolescence and replacement of products has the advantage of increasing volume of sales, but it carries with it the danger that consumers will be dissatisfied by the gap between expectation and the reality of product performance.

The introduction of strong consumer protection is a relatively new idea in the United States. For some years there have been bodies charged with regulating various aspects of industry and trade—for example the Federal Trade Commission, the Federal Communications Commission, and the Food and Drug Administration. But such bodies have traditionally been defenders of and apologists for the industries in question, rather than vigorous advocates of the interests of the consumer. The most outspoken consumer advocate in recent years has been a private individual, Ralph Nader, whose book *Unsafe at Any Speed* first exposed the dangers in contemporary automobile design and construction.

The growing strength of consumer indignation has led to the establishing of an Office of Consumer Affairs, a Consumer Protection Agency, and a Presidential enunciation of a 'Buyers Bill

of Rights'. Laws have been passed concerning truth in lending
and truth in packaging, and there is talk of others dealing with
truth in pricing and truth in warranties. Thus the pressure from
the public has forced a reluctant government to take action, and
business itself has recognised that in its own interests some
reforms are needed. However, private consumer groups feel
that the new legislation is not strong enough and not enforced
with sufficient vigour, and that the traditional slogan *caveat
emptor* or 'buyer beware' is still the soundest guiding principle
in the American market-place.

At the end of the 1960s environmental pollution suddenly became a major national issue. Industry has been exuding its
waste matter into the air and water with impunity for genera-
tions, and the emergence of this issue at this time appears to
have coincided with a number of authoritative statements concerning the extent of environmental pollution, and its possible
dangers to the survival of mankind. Major water bodies such
as Lake Erie have become incapable of sustaining normal
aquatic life and are even unsafe for bathing in places, and the
level of air pollution in large cities such as New York and Los
Angeles has become a potential public health hazard. Concern
for the environment has traditionally been limited to the possibility of exhaustion of sources of food, energy and materials,
but the new anti-pollution movement has been more concerned
with the earth's capacity to absorb the increasing amount of
waste matter which a modern industrial society is generating.

The early champions of the environmental crusade were on
the university campuses. But air and water pollution affects all
segments of society, and the affluent middle class soon combined
with student activists in opposition to pollution. The whole
nation has now become ecology conscious.

As with consumer protection, it took a public outcry to make
the government act in an area where some business freedom
would inevitably be infringed. The power to regulate polluters
and enforce specific standards was vested in the Clean Air Act
of 1963 and the Water Pollution Control Act of 1965, but there
was considerable reluctance to take major polluters such as the

giant steel corporations and off-shore oil operators to court. Consequently, very little came of this legislation. But mounting public concern led the Nixon Administration to take further steps to combat pollution, including the establishing of an Environmental Quality Council, a National Environmental Quality Act (1969), and the setting up of a large new Environmental Protection Agency in Washington. Whether there has really been a fundamental change in attitudes which have for so long rested on an essentially exploitive view of the natural environment is, however, as yet uncertain. And it also remains to be seen how far government is really prepared to go in enforcing compliance with new standards, particularly when some of the businesses concerned may be major contributors to political campaign funds.

4

How They Live

In the minds of the rest of the world the American way of life is usually associated with a high degree of affluence and material prosperity. For many nations it acts as a model, the desired end result of industrialisation under democratic government and the ultimate reward for hard work and sustained economic growth. Even in the Communist world the American way of life is viewed with a mixture of admiration and envy, and the achievement of something comparable is a frequently stated goal.

The average American is certainly better off in most respects than his counterpart in other countries, and the great majority of Americans enjoy a level of personal comfort and material

———

Roadside advertising billboards—an everyday scene in the city, as motels, service stations and restaurants compete for attention.

Waiting for the ride to school—the spacious station waggon and single-storey 'ranch-style' home epitomise American suburban living.

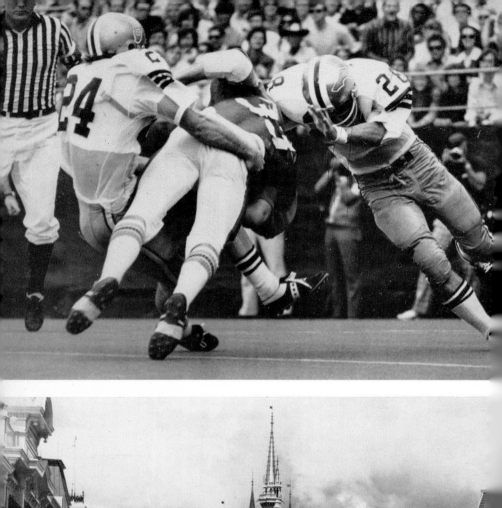

well-being which is available only to a small élite in most other parts of the world. However, there are aspects of life in which some Americans are less fortunately placed, and a substantial minority still cannot participate fully in many areas of the affluent society. How the average American lives is, of course, closely related to what he earns, the more so because of the poorly developed social services. A new car, a nice suburban home full of gadgets and appliances, plentiful food and drink, good schools and health care, and ample opportunities for leisure pursuits are readily available, to those able and willing to work for them.

THE FAMILY

The family is almost a sacred institution to Americans. It has always been thought of as a major source of national strength, with its solidarity tempered by the struggle for survival on the frontier and in the immigrant ghettos of the cities. By family in this context is meant the immediate family of mother, father and the children, with perhaps a small number of relatives.

The typical American family has three or four children (in 1970 the national average was 3·4 per family). The Americans

---

A college football game: heavily padded warriors playing out their ritual on artificial turf, under the surveillance of a striped-shirted referee.

Walt Disney World, Florida, the latest and greatest of the nation's amusement centres, where families can make an escape into a fantasy world.

F

tend to marry early, and most mothers have finished child-bearing by their middle twenties. American society is often described as a matriarchy, such is the importance of the mother, and it is common to describe national characteristics as being 'as American as motherhood or apple pie'. Although an increasing proportion of women are now going out to work, the place of the married woman is traditionally in the home with the children, and this is the role she is taught to expect and conform to. The competitive nature of the economic system means that men have to be highly job or career oriented, and in their recreational pursuits there is a strong emphasis on things like sport and hunting which emphasise masculinity and require male companions. This tends to strengthen the focal role of the mother in family life.

Although the American family is often pictured as doing things together—the family outing, the vacation trip or the back-yard barbecue—there are strong elements of separatism in the individual activities of family members. The men have their jobs, their leisure activities, and their clubs. The women have their responsibilities to the children and their own job if they have one, and participation in clubs, charity work, coffee parties and bridge mornings if they belong to the middle class. If husband and wife go out together in the evening, it is often to a social gathering or a cinema, neither of which encourages communication between marriage partners, and an evening at home in front of the TV hardly makes for conversation. The children are involved in sport and other school or peer-group activities, while in the summer they can be sent off to a camp, and as they grow up they may firmly reject parental values and mores. Thus many families are not closely knit groups, but rather a collection of individuals with their own largely separate lives who simply occupy the same dwelling and have a mutual economic interdependence.

For the majority of people, family life may well fulfil most if not all of their personal needs. But there appears to be a growing instability in the American family. One in every four marriages now ends in divorce, and in 1970 there were four divorcees in every hundred women over eighteen years of age compared with three in 1960. In 1971 almost 10 per cent of white families were headed by women (ie there was no husband, or he had left, died or been divorced) compared with 8·5 in 1950, but for Blacks the proportion has risen from less than 18 per cent to almost 30 per cent over the same period. Illegitimacy is on the increase, and now accounts for about 10 per cent of all live births compared with 4 per cent twenty years ago. Thus a broken home or a fatherless family is the environment in which an increasing number of American children grow up, and it is from this kind of background that a disproportionate number of delinquents, criminals and future unsuccessful marriage partners come.

Despite these trends, the importance of the family as the basic unit for the maintenance of economic security must not be overlooked. Generally, Americans would rather take care of their own than have them supported by the community or some government welfare programme. The income of most families is such as to enable them to do this to a large extent. There are families who cannot meet these needs, and break up as a partial consequence, and current development in the area of social services is aimed at strengthening the weak family unit and improving its economic self-sufficiency.

THE HOME

Almost two-thirds of the American families own their own homes, and the acquisition of a modern house in a good-class suburb is an important objective in the fulfilment of the American way of life. There are apartments for both rich and poor, and in some parts of the country (for example on the Florida coast) there is a boom in the construction of service apartments or 'condominiums' for sale. But the choice of most Americans is still a single-family residence.

The home rivals the automobile as the most conspicuous personal symbol of material well-being. Even when compared with other advanced industrial nations, such as those in north-west Europe, the house in America is generally spacious and extremely well equipped. The older houses within the cities often lack the drabness and monotony of the redbrick terraces of the nineteenth-century industrial cities of western Europe, though every major American city has its slums. And the suburban estates or 'subdivisions' are built with lower densities (often less than four houses to the acre), and with much greater variety of house design, than is the practice in Britain, for example. The median value of owner-occupied houses was $17,000 in 1970, and about two houses in five are valued at over $20,000. Average monthly rents are now about $100. In a typical American city a professional or managerial employee earning $15,000–20,000 might spend $250 a month on rental property or buy a house for $30,000–40,000.

The emphasis in the American housing market is very much on the middle classes, where the money is and where the status seekers are. In 1970 about one-third of all new single-family homes built was priced at over $30,000, whereas less than one in twenty were priced under $15,000. The construction industry has been very successful at mass producing homes with lots of space, with modern kitchens, and increasingly with built-in central heating and air conditioning. It has not been so successful in providing for the needs of the poor or those with relatively low incomes. This segment of society not only provides a less lucrative market less inclined to pay for the luxury increasingly built into a new home as standard equipment, but also finds it difficult to borrow money in the normal mortgage market.

It is difficult to estimate how many American families live in inadequate housing, as official figures vary according to the criteria used. Of the 70 million housing units in the country as a whole, about one in ten is substandard by virtue of lacking indoor plumbing or being in a dilapidated condition. Almost one in ten are overcrowded, having an average of more than one person per room. Although poor quality is usually associated with the inner city, this is as much a rural as an urban problem in the United States; the black farmhand in the south, for example, is probably as badly housed as any European peasant. However, considerable progress has been made with the improvement in housing conditions since the beginning of the 1950s.

With the private sector building very few houses for low income families, the options of such people are limited. They can occupy better houses vacated as others leave for the suburbs, thus improving their position absolutely if not relatively. They may be able to get a mortgage subsidised by the federal government through the Federal Housing Administration. Or they may be able to move into a public housing project. Public housing is the usual partial solution of the cities to the housing problem, but the projects have often been badly designed and located, and social conditions in many of them are little better than in the slums. The major city public housing projects are largely occupied by Blacks, who combine the disadvantage of a low income with that of a skin colour which prevents them from moving into much of white suburbia even if they could afford it. For the most part, housing is still strongly segregated along racial lines in the United States.

For an increasing number of middle- and low-income families unable to afford new houses, a 'mobile home' is the answer. This would be a superior caravan in Britain, designed to be used without a permanent foundation as a year-round dwelling when connected with utilities. Although mobile homes can cost as much as $35,000 in their most luxurious form, the typical unit 65 feet long and 12 feet wide would cost from $4,000 to $12,000, depending on equipment and interior. The unit is purchased and then set up on a site within a 'mobile home park', which in its appearance can vary from smart to squalid. Such is the demand for low-priced housing that the number of mobile homes delivered has doubled in the last five years; while the number of private housing units built has remained virtually the same.

An important feature of the American home is its multiplicity of gadgets, 'mod cons', labour-saving devices, and sources of electronic entertainment. Few trends so readily exemplify the

emergence of the affluent society as the increase in the ownership of electrical appliances in recent years, as indicated by the
figures below:

Item	Per cent of Homes	
	1953	*1971*
Air conditioners in rooms	1·3	40·6
Coffee-makers (percolators)	51·0	88·6
Dishwashers	3·0	26·5
Disposers for food waste	3·3	25·5
Driers, for clothes	3·6	44·6
Freezers (ie deep freeze)	11·5	31·2
Mixers (food)	29·7	82·4
Radios	96·2	99·8
Refrigerators	89·2	99·8
Television (black and white)	46·7	98·7
Television (colour)	nil	42·5
Toasters	70·9	92·6
Vacuum cleaners	59·4	92·0
Washers, for clothes	76·2	92·1

In addition, almost 50 million home hair driers were sold in
the 1960s and about half this number of electric carving knives.
Sales of record players and stereo systems have also been high.

Thus the ownership of what might be considered the basic
electrical appliances is now almost universal. Even a poor
family would be expected to have a television, a refrigerator,
an electric stove and a radio; poverty is always relative, and the
American poor are probably the most materially affluent in the
world. That so many people can afford these things is partly
because the large size of the American market has enabled
manufacturers to mass produce and hence cut costs. The manufacturer is constantly adding improvements, and as the well-off
replace the obsolete models the secondhand market distributes
them to poorer people.

The speed with which colour television has been adopted is a
dramatic illustration of the operation of the domestic consumer
market. In 1965 less than three homes in a hundred had such a

set, but the figure is now approaching one in two. Strong advertising predisposes the public to buy the product, its acquisition by friends or neighbours puts on extra pressure, and the relatively low cost of producing large numbers brings prices down to levels most people feel they can afford with the assistance of credit (the cheapest models cost about $300). Then quite soon it seems that everyone has one, and a luxury has become a necessity. Almost one family in three now has more than one television set, and the average family has five radios.

SHOPPING

Shopping habits, or marketing as it is usually called in the United States, are different in many respects from those of Europe. Except in the rural areas, and in parts of the metropolis where neighbourhood stores still survive, shopping is generally done in large supermarkets. These stock every type of food, milk and dairy produce, groceries, fish, poultry and meat, fruit and vegetables, soft drinks, and often also beer and wine. Non-food items such as soap powder and domestic cleaning requisites are also stocked. Most housewives shop just once a week for food, and even less frequently for certain items which can be deep frozen or otherwise stored. The quantity of goods purchased, and the location of the supermarkets or shopping centres, means that the use of an automobile is obligatory—to go to the shops on foot or pushing the baby in a pram as in Britain would be physically impossible for most housewives.

The average shopper's supermarket expenditures out of a $20 bill in 1960 and 1969 were:

Major categories	Dollars spent	
	1960	*1969*
Perishable foods	10.68	9.85
Other foods and grocery products	8.04	7.81
Non-foods	1.28	2.34
Total	20.00	20.00

Main individual items

Meat, fish and poultry	4.85	4.54
Produce (fruit and vegetables)	2.08	2.00
Dairy products	1.74	1.43
Canned foods	1.34	1.24
Frozen foods, including ice-cream	.97	1.00
Bakery products	1.04	.88
Beer	.88	.85
Tobacco products	.81	.79
Health and beauty aids	.53	.69
Cleaning supplies	.60	.56
Coffee and tea	.72	.53
Candy (sweets), cookies (biscuits), etc	.55	.52

Goods tend to be packaged in large quantities, on the assumption that people have adequate refrigeration space or other storage capacity. This kind of packaging also ensures that the customer will buy six bottles of his chosen brand of soft drink or beer, or a couple of dozen bread rolls, instead of single units of a product.

Most shops stock a vast range and choice of products. For example, in a supermarket patronised by these authors, there are twenty-four varieties of packaged cake mix on display, fifteen varieties of 'frosting' mix for icing cakes, twenty flavours of ice-cream and ten of sherbet. Speciality ice-cream parlours may offer as many as forty different flavours. Generally the fruit and vegetable section will have a great variety of products also, as they can be shipped in from all parts of the country, so what would otherwise be seasonal items are often available all the year round.

Virtually every type of food is pre-packaged, including fruit, vegetables, meat, bacon and bread. There are enumerable 'convenience' foods designed to save the housewife the time and effort of cooking, from instant breakfast products and instant vegetables and puddings to a wide variety of frozen complete meals or 'TV dinners' ready to be heated and eaten on tinfoil plates. The consumer habit of keeping products refrigerated for quite long periods means that various preservatives have to be used. Artificial colouring, sweetening and nutrients are frequently added to foods, in accordance with the American assumption that nature can always be improved upon. These practices include the injection of fat into bacon to increase its weight, and the 'tenderising' of poor quality meat by the injection of water or other substances. The use of artificial additives in food products is part of the current concern of the consumer protection movement.

Speciality shops such as bakeries, butchers and greengrocers are comparatively rare, though they can still be found in parts of the cities. In some areas dairies provide a delivery service, though most people buy their milk at the supermarket where it is cheaper. Neither supermarkets nor the speciality stores usually deliver, which is another reason why shopping is almost exclusively an automobile activity. Shopping in America is not a social event as it may be in Europe; shopping centres are seldom aesthetically attractive places and the stores are impersonal, and it is something to be accomplished as quickly as possible.

The larger towns and cities have department stores, branches of the national chains such as Woolworths and Sears Roebuck, and independent outlets for clothing and the wide range of consumer durables. The smaller towns are less well served, with a more limited range of shops, small branches of the chain stores, and the inevitable 'drug stores' selling pharmaceutical goods, toilet preparations, stationery and so on. The isolation of many towns in earlier times led to mail-order purchasing, and this is still used extensively all across the country. The main mail-order catalogue sales businesses are Sears Roebuck, Montgomery Ward and J. C. Penny. Most towns have an office where orders are placed and deliveries collected.

Whereas food prices are higher than in Europe, the price of clothing, appliances and other consumer goods tends to be lower, especially if the differences in earnings are taken into account. However, American products are often not up to European quality. They are manufactured down to a price established by the competitive process (in activities where there is true price competition), and durability is not a major selling point. European goods thus frequently have an aura of superior quality in America.

FOOD AND DRINK

The average American consumes about 3,250 calories of food each day, which is a little more than in most advanced industrial nations and half as much again as in India and China. Per capita annual consumption of meat in pounds is about 240, comparable with Argentina, Australia, New Zealand and Uraguay as the other largest meat eaters, and twice as high as in many western European countries. The United States is a major meat producer, and incomes are high enough to put some kind of meat on the table of almost every family. The consumption of cereals (140lb per person each year) is consequently low, being less than half the figure in much of the undeveloped world and slightly lower than in most advanced nations.

Breakfast is early, as shops and offices as well as factories are usually open by 8.00 am. Cereals, eggs and bacon may form part of the menu, but doughnuts and hot pastries are also popular, as are hot cakes or pancakes served with maple syrup, often accompanied by bacon and sausage. Instant breakfast foods are becoming increasingly popular, taking the form of powder stirred in milk. Coffee is almost invariably the breakfast beverage, perhaps accompanied by orange juice.

Lunch is normally between 12.00 and 1.00. It usually consists either of sandwiches, perhaps served with potato chips (ie crisps) and pickles, or of hamburgers with 'French fries' (ie chips). A wide variety of sandwiches are made at home or are available for sale, and there are many cold meats (cold cuts) and sausages produced for this purpose.

The main cooked meal is usually in the evening, the most popular meats being beef and pork. Lamb and veal are eaten much less frequently. Good cuts of meat are expensive, and many families use chicken or ground meat as a substitute.

Chicken is usually fried or baked, and ground meat is offered in a variety of forms including meat loaf and the inevitable hamburgers. A small green salad is generally served either with or before the main course, and various dressings are produced to accompany it. Typical desserts would be ice-cream, sherbet, or a plate 'fruit pie'.

Cooking outdoors in the back yard or on a trip is common. This is done on a portable grill or barbecue stove, and will generally consist of hamburgers, hot dogs or steak. In summer a suburban family may do this once a week, the husband taking responsibility for the cooking as befits the descendants of the hardy frontiersmen.

A wide variety of soft drinks is available and consumed in vast quantities. The best-known is of course Coca Cola, but other similar beverages are almost as popular. Beer is consumed by men, with an enthusiasm equalling that of any Europeans with the possible exception of the Germans; American beer is of the light lager type, and is almost invariably purchased in 'six-packs' of cans or (less frequently now) bottles. Scotch whisky is a popular spirits drink, but many Americans prefer their own whisky—Bourbon. Considerable quantities of wine are produced, the main vineyards being in California and (less important) New York State. American wines are inexpensive, but the average European palate can probably adjust to them fairly easily and find at least a few sources of unexpected pleasure.

For eating out, certain types of restaurants and foods tend to be ubiquitous from coast to coast. The most frequently found restaurants are the 'drive-in' kind providing food to be taken away to eat, and the chain or franchise establishments where the same basic menu can be found in any one branch in hundreds of different cities. Typical offerings of the drive-in restaurants are hamburgers, hot dogs, French fries, fried chicken, pizza, and fried shrimp or other fish. In the sit-down restaurants there are the most common kinds of meat cuts, probably some fish, a selection of sandwiches, and the usual beverages and desserts.

Most American food is 'homogenised' or standardised, with its quality a highly predictable mediocre. The major cities have the most varied offerings; for example in New York Italians, Hungarians, Germans, Puerto Ricans, Chinese and others have transplanted their cooking along with other aspects of their culture, and still live in their own neighbourhoods where the ingredients for their own special foods are readily available.

There are some local and regional variations and specialities. On the north-west coast seafood is popular, including salmon, halibut, trout and shellfish. In the mountain states there is an abundance of fresh-water fish. In the south-west food is frequently barbecued, but the most distinctive regional specialisation here comprises the Mexican dishes of tacos, enchiladas, tortillas, tamales and chile con carne. The plains produce excellent beefsteak, while the mid-western cities show the ethnic influence in their cooking—German in Chicago and Milwaukee, Polish in Detroit and Cleveland. In New England seafood is plentiful, particularly lobster and clams, and other local favourites are maple syrup and cranberries. In the middle Atlantic states the Pennsylvania Dutch country inhabited by the Amish and Mennonites is a distinctive region with a German flavour, offering such local specialities as 'shoofly' pie (made from molasses and crumbs), apple butter, and scrapple. Elsewhere pecan pie and pumpkin pie are reflections of the local availability of certain ingredients.

The South is perhaps the most distinctive food region. Hominy grits (a type of corn-based porridge) is usually served with breakfast, and hot bread 'biscuits', rolls and cornbread are available at other meals. Fried chicken and ham are popular, and ham or salt pork may be used to flavour vegetables. The deep south is the home of collard greens, black-eyed peas, candied yams and 'dirty' rice (rice with beans). Florida offers a wide variety of fruit, vegetables and seafood, and there is good Cuban cooking in Miami and Tampa.

HEALTH AND MEDICAL CARE

The United States spends over 70 billion dollars on health care each year. This is about 7 per cent of the Gross National Product (the highest proportion of any nation in the world), compared with about 5 per cent in Britain. There are over 7,000 hospitals with a total of over 1,660,000 beds, and these include some of the most advanced medical educational and research institutions in the world. There are almost 350,000 doctors (or physicians), almost 120,000 dentists, and 700,000 nurses. Supporting this system of health care is a huge pharmaceutical industry which spends millions of dollars each year on the development of new drugs, and an insurance industry which provides the majority of Americans with some protection against the costs of care.

With these vast resources, the United States might be expected to be the healthiest nation on earth. There have certainly been dramatic improvements in health during the present century, with some diseases, such as polio and diphtheria, almost completely eliminated, while others, like tuberculosis and measles, are far less common than they used to be. Average life expectancy is now over seventy years, compared with less than fifty at the turn of the century. During the past quarter of a century the rate of infant mortality has been more than halved, maternal mortality has been greatly reduced, and the death-rate from many diseases has gone down sharply. Improvements in medical technology, and in particular the development of new drugs, have had a clear and measurable impact on the nation's level of physical and mental health.

However, the health of the Americans compares unfavourably with that enjoyed by many advanced industrial nations. And in some areas the relative position of the United States is worsening. Infant mortality is a widely accepted indicator of a society's standard of health, and the figures for the United States are especially revealing. In 1950 the country ranked fifth in the world (ie there were only four countries with a lower rate of infant deaths), in 1955 it was eighth, in 1960 twelfth, and by the end of the 1960s it had fallen to twenty-third according to a United Nations report. In life expectancy seventeen countries have a higher figure than the United States for men, and ten have a higher figure for women. In maternal mortality six other countries have lower rates than the United States. More than a dozen countries have lower incidence of ulcers, diabetes, cirrhosis of the liver, hypertension and accidents. In short, the richest nation in the world lags behind many other advanced industrial nations in its health levels, and the gap appears to be widening.

The standard of American medical science cannot explain this, for the best care available is the best in the world. Neither is it explained by lack of personnel, for the rates of physicians, dentists and nurses to population are exceeded by very few other countries. The reason lies largely in the organisation of medical care, which is provided on a fee-for-service basis. As the price of medical care has risen faster than incomes, an increasing proportion of the American people are finding the cost of keeping well or getting cured too high for them to meet.

The provision of health care in the United States has to be viewed as a business, not as a public service. The doctor or dentist is a private businessman who makes a profit by providing a personal service, in just the same way as a lawyer or a real-estate agent. He charges a fee for an office visit and for his professional services. He is more likely to be a specialist than a general practitioner, and it is unlikely that he will make house-calls because he can make more money by having the patients come to him. The fact that he is usually a highly successful businessman is indicated by his annual earnings, which now average over $40,000 a year.

In choosing where to practise, doctors tend to locate themselves where the financial prospects are greatest. Thus the larger metropolitan centres have twice as many doctors in relation to population as rural areas, where incomes are lower. Country doctors tend to be older and less well trained than their city counterparts, and 130 counties have no doctors at all. The richer states have more doctors than the poorer states; for example, New York and Massachusetts have over 200 physicians per 100,000 residents, while the rate in most southern states is less than 100. The inner city ghetto areas have far fewer doctors than the middle-class suburbs. The more physicians there are in relation to population, the lower the infant and maternal mortality rates, the lower the levels of infectious disease, and the higher the life expectancy.

More than one hospital in five in the United States is run for private profit. The rest may be subsidised to some extent by local, state or federal funds, but they still have to cover expenses. This they do by charging the patient for room and board, and for the various services rendered within the hospital other than those of the physician, anaesthetist, surgeon, and so on.

The almost total reliance on the physician is an important feature of American medical care. To relinquish any of their functions to nurses or other medical auxiliary workers means a loss of potential income. This helps to explain the general absence of midwives, home health visitors, and social workers, who are used extensively in health care in many other countries. The practice of the doctor performing even the most routine of treatments is a major reason for the high cost of medical care.

The average cost of a spell in hospital in the United States is now about $600. Costs per day are $70 for the nation as a whole, and almost $100 in some of the most expensive states such as California and Massachusetts. A few minutes in a doctor's office can cost ten dollars; with a specialist it may be twenty-five. Costs of medical care are increasing at a far greater rate than the general cost of living.

Five out of six Americans are covered by some kind of health insurance. But in very few cases is this coverage comprehensive, and generally a substantial proportion of the cost has to be met by the patient. The Medicare and Medicaid programme introduced a few years ago to help the aged require a monthly payment, and the patient still has to pay the first sixty dollars or so of hospital expenses. The poor can get some medical attention through the welfare system, but it is generally of an inferior kind, and a cost is exacted in terms of the loss of human dignity often associated with obtaining services for which the recipient cannot pay a fee. The lower a person's income, the less often he receives medical care.

The United States is the only advanced industrial nation without some system of national health service or insurance. But pressure for this kind of arrangement is growing. Thus far public intervention has been strongly resisted by the American Medical Association, which acts as major protector of doctors' financial interests, and by the private medical insurance industry. Some improved medical insurance system seems inevitable, because the middle classes are now suffering greatly from rising costs, but it is at present highly unlikely that this, or the provision of medical care itself, will be removed from private hands and taken over by the federal government. 'Socialised medicine', as its opponents shrewdly call it, is by definition un-American, and not even such a basic human need as adequate health care is yet strong enough to transcend the basic American values of private enterprise and individual economic freedom.

\

Slum housing. About one American family in ten lives in inadequate housing, like this wooden shack in the South.

Migrant farm workers in New York State, some of the rural poor who work long hours in insecure employment for low wages.

SOCIAL WELFARE

The provision of social welfare services in the United States has its foundation in the Social Security Act of 1935 and its subsequent amendments. This provides funds for selected programmes, rather than establishing a comprehensive federal welfare system. Social security covers three types of services: (1) a social insurance programme which aims to establish a minimum standard of living by protecting against the loss of earning capacity; (2) a programme of public assistance to help people in economic distress, generally known as 'welfare'; (3) a very limited programme of health services.

In the first category, about nine-tenths of the working population are covered by the Old Age, Survivors and Disability Insurance programme. Both employees and employers make compulsory contributions to the scheme, from which retired or disabled workers and their dependents or survivors receive cash benefits.

Unemployment compensation is provided under a different scheme. Each state administers its own plan, with its own

———

Early settlers in the New World: a re-enactment of the first Thanksgiving, at Plymouth, Massachusetts, where the Pilgrim Fathers landed.

Modern American explorer in another new world—how astronaut David R. Scott lived and worked for a while, on the Apollo 15 lunar landing.

qualifications and payments, but the cost is met by the federal government and the state schemes are supervised by the Bureau of Employment Security in the Department of Labor. Unemployment compensation is far from comprehensive, and perhaps as many as a third of all workers are not covered. All states have workmen's compensation programmes providing protection against work-connected injuries and death, but again not everyone is covered. Only four states operate sickness benefit schemes, combined with their unemployment compensation programmes. There are no maternity benefits or family allowances.

The second programme under the Social Security Act provides for general public assistance, or aid to those with no other sources of income. This is financed by the states. There are also types of specific assistance: old age assistance, aid to the blind, aid to the permanently and totally disabled, and aid to families with dependent children. The federal government shares the cost of these programmes with the states, but it does not administer them. The Act allows the individual states wide latitude in the provision of assistance and in its administration, and each state decides the conditions under which needy people may receive help and how much they get. This means that payments vary greatly from state to state and city to city and generally, the lowest levels of public assistance on any programme are in the south, and the highest are in California and the north-east.

The health services available under the Social Security Act are extremely limited. The states can get federal money for medical assistance to persons not able to meet their own medical bills, but this is no guarantee that any poor person can obtain treatment, for there are many practical and institutional problems to overcome. Since July 1966 a voluntary contributory system of health insurance, the Medicare and Medicaid programmes, has been provided for people over 65 years of age.

Attempts were made to fill some of the gaps in the provision of social services under the Social Security Act by the Economic Opportunity Act passed in 1964. This was part of the Great Society programme initiated by the Kennedy Administration with the aim of preventing and eventually abolishing poverty.

It included youth programmes devised to help people from low-income groups to receive education or job training. The Act also provided federal funds for various public and private organisations to combat poverty through the rehabilitation of slum neighbourhoods. One of the best-known community action programmes is Head Start, which prepares children from poor families for school, and incidentally provides many of them with their first medical examinations and health care and their first nutritional meals. The Act also provided for loans to small businesses, and offered some job training or retraining for the unemployed or persons on welfare. Another programme is VISTA (Volunteers in Service to America), through which young volunteer workers help with rehabilitation in the slums and rural poverty areas. The Office of Economic Opportunity, responsible for the entire 'war on poverty', was made part of the Executive Office of the President, and is not under the Department of Health, Education and Welfare which administers social security. Most of the anti-poverty programmes are now (1973) under review, and likely to be completely reorganised.

As well as the federal and state schemes, there are hundreds of private organisations and agencies providing assistance to the needy. Some of the larger ones are completely independent, and run their own fund drives. However, many rely for their money on the United Fund (or United Way), which launches a large annual campaign for financial assistance to charity in communities all across the nation. Individuals contribute to the fund on a voluntary basis, and the money collected is shared among a variety of local agencies or programmes.

The present provision of social services in the United States is far from comprehensive. Compared with that of many other advanced industrial nations, it is fragmented and uncoordinated. Some contingencies of life are covered, while others are ignored or assumed to be the responsibility of the individual rather than of government. To many Americans the whole idea of welfare is seen as a waste of taxpayers' hard-earned dollars in supporting the indigent, and a step on the slippery path to Socialism. The most likely innovation in the near future is a guaranteed minimum family income of very modest proportions.

CRIME AND LAW ENFORCEMENT

What is generally described as the 'law and order' issue is very important in contemporary life in America. Crime rates have been rising rapidly in recent years, and this has been accompanied by growing public concern for the safety of lives and property. Some special categories of crime, including draft resistance, the use of marijuana, the deception of consumers, and infringements of laws for the protection of the environment, raise political as well as legal issues. The riots which occurred in some cities in the latter part of the 1960s indicated that there is a real danger of major civil disorders among the deprived minority populations, and the political activism of these groups and of some of the students' generation occupies a precarious position on the edge of the law. Added to all this are some genuine doubts as to whether the police are efficient and sensitive enough to deal with the various different dimensions of illegal behaviour in contemporary America, and some equally serious doubts as to whether the courts are dispensing justice impartially and whether the prisons are performing the true function of correctional institutions.

There is no disputing the fact that America has a serious crime problem. The following figures give some information on the rates of major crimes, as known to the police:

Type of Crime	Number of offences (1,000s) 1970	Rate per 100,000 people 1970	Increase in rate (per cent) 1960–70
Violent Crime			
Murder and non-negligent manslaughter	16	8	56
Forcible rape	37	18	95
Burglary	348	172	186
Aggravated assault	330	162	92

Property Crime

Burglary	2,169	1,068	113
Larceny $50 and over	1,746	859	204
Auto theft	921	454	150

The total number of offences in the above categories has risen from just over 2 million in 1960 to 5½ million in 1970, the number of violent crimes has risen from 285,000 to 731,000, and the number of crimes against property has gone up from 1,729,000 to 4,837,000. These figures do not include crimes unknown to the police, and the proportion of certain minor offences not reported may be very high. Nor do they include what is sometimes known as 'white-collar crime'—fraud, embezzlement, corruption of public officials, and crimes against the consumer or the environment.

Although figures on crime rates are generally not accurate enough for useful international comparisons to be made, the high level of violent crime is a distinguishing feature of the United States when compared with other advanced nations. The present murder rate of about 15,000 a year is thirty times the number in Britain; there are as many murders in the city of Detroit or on Manhattan Island in a year as in the whole of Britain. Two-thirds of all murders are committed by guns, which the Americans possess in their homes in large numbers. A particularly serious trend is the number of police officers killed in the line of duty, which has risen from less than 50 in 1960 to about 130 annually today.

Crime tends to be concentrated in the cities, and in general the bigger the city the higher the crime rate. Cities with over a quarter of a million people have eight times the rate of violent crimes than rural areas, and five times the rate of property crimes. The highest rates are in the inner city ghettos, where the social conditions and economic deprivation create breeding grounds for crime. Suburban crime rates are only about one-fifth of those of the inner city, but the rate in the suburbs has risen more rapidly in recent years.

Law enforcement can be divided into three parts: apprehension, prosecution and punishment. Of all the offences known to the police, only about one in five leads to an apprehension or arrest. About one person in four charged of a crime is found guilty as charged. Punishment can range from probation or a small fine to a prison term which may exceed life expectancy by a wide margin.

The investigation of crimes and the arrest of suspects is the job of the police. There are thousands of different police forces in the United States, including municipal police, county police, state police, sheriffs, constables, marshals, federal agents, and other kinds of special police. In the major city police departments, which deal with most of the nation's crime, highly sophisticated techniques of criminal detection have been developed, involving the use of advanced computer technology. The American police are in general rather more aggressive and 'trigger-happy' than their counterparts in most western European nations. It is difficult to view them as entirely non-political today, as most policemen are drawn from blue-collar and 'ethnic' backgrounds which in the current era of social activism leads them on occasions to lose their objectivity in dealing with peace demonstrators, dissident Blacks, and others who oppose the existing establishment.

When a suspect is apprehended the district attorney's office decides whether the facts gathered by the police warrant a prosecution. In certain circumstances a case has to be made to a grand jury before the decision to go to trial or not is made. For all but the most trivial offence, the Constitution guarantees the accused a trial before a jury of his peers if he chooses. Attorneys have the right to reject jurors, and can thus eliminate persons who seem likely to be biased or unsympathetic to their point of view. The court is presided over by a judge, who passes sentence after conviction. Minor offences may be dealt with by a judge alone, or by a justice of the peace. A growing problem, particularly in the major city courts, is the delay in getting a suspect to trial in the face of a backlog of cases.

There are over 350,000 persons in 'correctional institutions' or all kinds. About 20,000 are in Federal prisons, which are usually the better-run institutions and range from maximum security bastions to prisons without walls. Almost 200,000 are in state prisons, which can vary greatly in quality and in the degree of correctional training given. About 160,000 are in the 4,000 or so city and county jails, where conditions tend to be most primitive. A major current criticism of the American prison system is that it does not rehabilitate the criminal. It is certainly true that many institutions do not have psychiatrists and other necessary trained personnel to deal with the emotional problems that the convicted often bring in with them, and that few of the so-called correctional officers (guards) have any training. It is also true that a proportion approaching half of all inmates commit another crime within five years of release. Most informed opinion now supports a fundamental overhaul of the American prison system, with the replacement of incarceration by rehabilitation as the predominant strategy.

THE STATUS OF WOMEN

From an early age the female American is socialised in the home and at school towards the acceptance of the traditional role of wife and mother. But as more and more women take jobs, and as the composition of the female labour force changes, some uncertainty is arising with respect to the woman's role in American society.

Since 1950 the proportion of women at work has risen from less than one-third to 43 per cent. While the proportion of single women at work has gone up only slightly, the proportion of married women with jobs has almost doubled. Married women now make up almost two-thirds of the female workforce, compared with only just over half in 1950. Three-quarters of the women at work are employed full time, most of them because they have to support a fatherless family or supplement the husband's income to provide for education, unexpected medical bills, or simply to raise the family living standard. But it is by no means always a case of economic necessity; a recent Department of Labor survey showed that one-fifth of women questioned were at work for 'social or psychological reasons'.

Employment opportunities for women are more restricted than for men. This is partly because women often have less education and training, but it is also because certain occupations are the traditional preserve of the male. Compared with many other industrialised nations, women are poorly represented in the professions. For example, in the medical profession the proportion of women is only 7 per cent while in the Soviet Union 70 per cent of physicians are women and in Britain nearly 25 per cent. Only 22 per cent of the faculty and other professional staff in institutes of higher learning are women, even though almost 30 per cent of the PhDs awarded nationally are to women, and in the major universities the proportion of women is very much lower. Only 4 of the 500 or so federal judges are women.

Women also have less political representation than their counterparts in many other western democracies. Only 1 of the 100 senators is a woman, and only 11 of the 435 members of the House of Representatives. In appointive positions, less than 2 per cent of the 3,800 top federal jobs are held by women.

Even when the college-educated woman gets a job she is likely to earn less than a man with similar training. A survey in 1968 found that the average woman college graduate earned about $6,700 a year compared with $11,800 for men. In general, women are three times less likely than men to earn over $5,000 a year in full-time work, and only 3 per cent of women as against 28 per cent of men earn over $10,000 a year.

As more women have gone to college, the lack of opportunities and the practical difficulty of doing a job in a profession while looking after a house and family are causing many educated married women to feel dissatisfied with their social role. Participation in the local club life, drinking coffee, exchanging gossip, and doing the occasional charitable work are found to be no substitute for professional activity. Jobs like teaching, which a woman can combine relatively easily with normal family life, are few.

An outcome of the growing dissatisfaction of women with their traditional role is the Women's Liberation Movement, which has emerged during the past few years. Members of the movement generally hold that women are discriminated against in employment and other walks of life, that because certain kinds of behaviour and certain occupations have been expected of them from birth women find it difficult to become autonomous individuals, and that most men treat women merely as sexual objects. Although the 'Women's Lib' movement is very small, its impact has been quite dramatic. Some of the more extreme have engaged in the ritual burning of bras, and there is a trend towards the abandonment of this undergarment as a symbol of sexual emancipation. Whatever the American male may feel about 'Women's Lib'—and in general he is unsympathetic to the cause—there are some manifestations which he cannot ignore.

HOW THEY END THEIR LIVES

Whatever kind of life an American lives, it will eventually end in death. Some cynics observe that what money the doctors and hospitals do not get will be taken by the funeral business. The disposal of the dead is certainly very expensive, for in 1970 the average cost of a funeral was about $950 according to the National Funeral Directors Association. As in so many other aspects of American life, business has responded to a need backed up by increasing purchasing power, by providing a very elaborate service with various distinctive embellishments, which the consumer is either happy to purchase or finds it difficult to avoid.

The centre of the business is the 'funeral home'. The casket (coffin) accounts for a large part of the funeral expense, and can cost anything from $500 to $4,000. In most cases there is a ritual viewing of the deceased within the casket prior to burial, and this requires various cosmetic treatments. Watertight caskets, embalming, deep freezing, and other preservative practices have an obvious appeal to Americans, who appreciate the triumph of technology over the natural course of events.

Another item of expense is the cemetery plot. These can vary from $25 for a small one in a rural church cemetery to well over $1,000 for a plot with a cement vault in a private city cemetery. The majority of Americans may now own their own plots prior to death.

It is very difficult to arrange an inexpensive funeral. Cremation is rare, accounting for only about 5 per cent of all disposals, but the practice is growing because it is much less costly than the more conventional method. However, many Americans are reluctant to do without the elaborate care and ritual which the funeral business has developed.

5

How They Learn

THE American educational system has three main divisions: elementary schools, secondary schools and institutions of higher learning. In each there is both a public and a private sector. Elementary schools take children up to the age of about fourteen; there are almost 70,000 public schools and about 15,000 non-public. Secondary schools take fourteen- to eighteen-year-olds; there are over 23,000 of these in public systems and 4,600 non-public. Institutions of higher education include junior or community colleges, four-year colleges and universities, and graduate and professional schools; private institutions (1,440) outnumber public (930). Over 50 million Americans attend school, and a further 7·5 million are enrolled in higher education.

THE ORGANISATION OF PUBLIC EDUCATION

The right to free public education is an important American principle. The public education system is organised through local school districts. It is divorced from national government and there are no uniform standards of education maintained across the country as a whole. There are almost 27,000 school districts, most being town or township units, and they vary considerably in size. Public elementary and secondary schools rely mainly on local taxes for their financing, though since 1965 there has been some state and federal support.

Because of economic differences, the level of education offered can vary considerably from one district to another. In general, the more money a child's parents earn, the more will be spent on his school, despite some efforts at public compensatory expenditure to upgrade schools in poor areas. In 1971 the average public school expenditures per pupil amounted to $858, but this rose to over $1,000 in New York, New Jersey, Washington DC, Massachusetts, Minnesota and Alaska. It fell to under $700 in many southern states, and as low as $489 in Alabama, even though the poorer states often spend a greater share of all their income on education than the richer states.

Within the major cities there can be extreme differences in educational expenditures, as between the affluent white middle-class suburbs which demand good schools and can pay for them, and the inner city with its ghetto, its poverty, and a population less interested in education or lacking influence in the school district. The inner-city schools often have obsolete and over-crowded buildings with inadequate equipment and staff. There may be language problems, arising from the influx of immigrants from Puerto Rico (especially in New York City) and Mexico, and of southern Blacks with poor verbal skills. The schools in the suburbs generally offer the better programme, in well-equipped buildings staffed by well-qualified teachers. On average, inner-city schools have about 35 staff (including teachers, administrators, domestic help, etc) per 1,000 pupils, whereas the suburban schools have roughly twice as many.

There are also contrasts between rural and urban school districts. Many rural districts are either too poor or too small to provide quality education. There are still about 4,000 one-teacher elementary schools in rural America.

The educational system in the individual school district is run by an elected school board. This is supposed to ensure community control, and parents can exercise further influence on the schools through the PTA (Parent Teacher Association), to which over 12 million parents throughout the nation belong. The majority of school board members are businessmen, farmers or professional people. They are overwhelmingly WASP (White Anglo-Saxon Protestant), their average age is almost fifty, and there are few women.

Given the composition of the average school board, it is not surprising that they tend to be conservative. They believe strongly in local control and firmly resist the federal intervention which some educators see as needed for the improved co-ordination of public education. They also tend to support business-oriented values and the capitalist political philosophy. This local control of schools means that the nature of the teaching material and hence what the child can learn are influenced by local beliefs. An extreme example of this is the continuing reluctance to teach evolution in parts of the South where it conflicts with fundamentalist religious dogma. More common is the way in which local school boards can protect children from exposure to literature regarded as 'undesirable' on moral or political grounds.

About 10 per cent of the total educational staff in America is engaged in full-time administration. They are the policy makers, and the school superintendent or chief administrator holds the key position in each school district. He may be elected by the people or appointed by the school board, and will usually have had college and teaching experience, and training in educational administration. Many school principals and teachers have little control over what is taught, as this is in the hands of the superintendent. Although about three-quarters of the teaching profession are women, administration is almost exclusively a male occupation, and men also hold most of the principal posts.

As a partial result of the decentralisation of public education and the lack of co-ordination, numerous voluntary educational associations have come into existence. These include 500 regional and national associations, about 150 college professional societies, and 50 religious educational associations. Their main function is the maintenance of standards, by such means as the accreditation of schools and teacher-training institutions and the certification of teachers. The organisation which dominates all others is the National Educational Association. This is neither an official public body nor representative of the people as a private organisation, but its influence may well be greater than that of any other group including the US Office of Education.

In 1971 over $60 billion were spent on public education in the United States. Most of this came from state and local sources, but $6.5 billion was federal money. The elementary and secondary schools together accounted for $43 billion, the rest going to higher education.

THE SCHOOLS

All states except Mississippi require that children attend school. However, state laws vary as to the ages and circumstances of compulsory attendance. In most states formal schooling must begin by the age of seven and continue to sixteen.

Depending on the state, the public elementary and secondary schools can provide education from as early as age five to as late as eighteen. Children can enrol for kindergarten when they are five, though in some states this is optional. The kindergarten classes meet for about two to three hours a day, and provide the content equivalent of a nursery school programme in Britain. There are excellent private 'pre-schools' for those who can afford them, taking children from ages three to five. In some poverty areas the Head Start programme prepares disadvantaged children for entry into school.

Formal education for most children begins in the elementary or 'grade' school. The class of each year is a grade, and the six-year-old enrols in Grade 1 where he first learns the basic reading and writing skills. The elementary school includes Grades 1 to 8 in most parts of the country. At about fourteen years of age the child enters the secondary system or 'high school' terminating in Grade 12, or 'junior high' for Grades 9 and 10 and high school for the final two grades. In 1970 the average years completed at school by Americans aged twenty-five or over was about twelve.

The national ratios of pupils per teacher in 1970 were 24·3 in elementary schools and 18·9 in secondary schools in the public sector. About two-thirds of the teachers hold bachelor degrees, and about a quarter have master degrees; less than 1 per cent have no degree. The high proportion with degrees is explained by the fact that the training of teachers is for the most part done in universities, for there are no teacher-training colleges. The average teacher earns about $9,300 a year. Apart from Alaska, where all wages and salaries are high, the best-paid teachers are in New York State and California, while the lowest are in Mississippi. There are now just over 2 million teachers in the country as a whole.

American schools vary enormously. Some in the rural areas are staffed by a single teacher. In the cities and suburban areas they can be vast institutions with perhaps 2,000 students, a large staff of teachers and professional administrators, and with timetables planned by computer. Most high schools employ counsellors or social workers, whose responsibility is to advise on the academic and personal difficulties a student can encounter. One problem of current concern is the use of drugs in schools, which appears to be growing rapidly as a result of their ready availability and the strong 'peer group' pressures to conform which exist in the American youth sub-culture. Belonging to a group is very important, and great prestige is attached to certain activities. For boys athletic prowess brings status, particularly to those occupying leadership positions on the football team, and equivalent positions for girls would be those of 'cheer leader'. Extra-curricular activity is generally dominated by the school band, which provides a vital accompaniment to sporting events and local community festivities. Almost all American schools are coeducational. Uniforms are rarely required.

Almost one school in five is private, with entry dependent on the payment of fees. Most of the private schools are Roman Catholic, and (because constitutionally public schools cannot be religious) these 'parochial schools' are important to people who favour a religious content in education. Parochial schools tend to exist alongside public schools rather than compete with them. Many are experiencing increasing financial difficulty, as they cannot be directly assisted from public funds and parents are finding it hard to pay the rising costs. In some parts, particularly in the South, private schools are means for Whites to keep their children out of public schools which are now racially integrated. A distinctive type of private school is the military academy—a boarding school organised on military lines.

There are various supplementary educational schemes, most of them federally funded, and designed to help disadvantaged children and high school 'drop-outs' with further education or job training. There are also university extension courses, offering programmes ranging from home management to farming methods. Indian Reservations have their own school systems, with children often boarding because of the long distances from school to home.

Educational achievement is always a difficult thing to measure, but some facts may be offered briefly. While a century ago one out of five Whites and four out of five Blacks in America were illiterate, almost everyone can now read and write, illiteracy rates are 1 per cent and 3·6 per cent respectively. Performance in the armed forces induction mental test is a good indicator of basic educational skills; nationally about one young man in five failed in the 1960s. Comparing American education with that of other nations, the International Study of Achievement in Mathematics showed American students to have one of the poorest performances of all the developed nations studied. There is a growing feeling in educational circles that the American school system may not be teaching its children as effectively as possible.

To understand this, one must appreciate that education in the usual sense is not necessarily the primary aim of the American school. Its main purpose is stamping the American character on its children. The part which the schools played in the assimilation of the sons and daughters of the alien immigrants in the nineteenth century was very important in welding such diverse people into a nation, for without some means of imbuing them with the values of the dominant culture and giving them a sense of patriotism and of belonging to America it is difficult to see how national unity could have been achieved. But the needs of the twentieth century, and of the complex modern technological society, are somewhat different, and the schools have been slow to respond to some of these new demands.

HIGHER EDUCATION

There are 2,400 colleges or universities in America, with over 7 million students. These institutions range from small community colleges with only a few dozen students to the great state universities with more than 50,000 students spread over more than one campus. Conditions for admission vary considerably; some colleges accept only those of the highest ability, while others take almost anyone who has graduated from high school regardless of ability. A university or college education for all who can benefit from it is an American ideal, and a degree has now become a necessary qualification for most professional and managerial jobs.

At present there are about 1,500 four-year colleges and 850 junior colleges. Almost 500 of the four-year colleges offer work up to the masters degree level, and about 230 grant PhDs. Twelve of them are federally controlled (ie military and government service schools), about 420 are state controlled, about 350 come under local government, and the rest are private. A breakdown on religious lines shows almost 500 Protestant, 300 Catholic, and most of the rest non-denominational. About 500 are exclusively male or female, and a few are still predominantly attended by Blacks.

The private institutions are supported by endowments, tuition fees and grants. The public colleges—state, municipal and community—are financed largely by taxes. Tuition fees in the public institutions are generally lower than in the private ones, where they can exceed $2,000 a year. State colleges usually charge higher fees for out-of-state students, thus encouraging attendance at the local institution.

The arrangement of degree courses is often different from

H

that in western Europe. Universities operate on a 'quarter' or 'semester' system, and the academic year is made up of either three quarters (four including the summer quarter) of ten study weeks, or two semesters of about three months. Students take courses for a quarter or semester rather than for the whole year. Each course is given a 'credit' of three, four or five hours, depending on the duration of class meetings each week, and the student has to amass a given number of credit hours to obtain a degree. Tuition is generally more highly structured than in Europe, with courses having a designated textbook which students are expected to read, although students often have a wide range of choice within which to design their own programmes. For the first two years they are usually required to take classes in 'General Studies' (roughly equivalent to sixth-form work in Britain); in the third and fourth year students are expected to 'major' in a particular subject. The undergraduate educational experience is likely to be more varied and more superficial than in most European countries.

First year students are known as 'freshmen', second year 'sophomores', third year 'juniors' and final year 'seniors'. Classes can range in size from a handful of students in a special final-year topic to many hundreds in an introductory freshman course. Because of the large classes and the lack of individual supervision which are inevitable in an institution of 20,000 to 30,000 students, there is little personal contact between students and teachers (called 'faculty'). Students are given identification numbers, and often are not known individually to the teacher but as entries on a class role printed out by a computer. Students get personal advice from departmental programme advisers or general counsellors. In many courses examination is by 'objective' testing, comprising multiple-choice questions, and not by essay-type answers, and these are usually marked or 'graded' by student assistants or by the computer.

It is in the graduate schools that the real strength of American higher education is to be found. Whereas the education provided at the bachelor level is often of poor quality, the American graduate system produces some of the world's greatest scholars, scientists, and technologists. Graduate schools cater for far greater numbers than in any other nation, and have carefully designed programmes to give rigorous training in subject matter and research methods. Like the undergraduate programme, they can vary greatly in quality, but the best have no equal anywhere in the world.

The larger four-year colleges offer a far wider range of courses than in Europe. They can include such topics as pig-rearing, golf, horse riding, theatre, and home economics, as well as the more conventional academic subjects. Many junior colleges offer vocational training in such fields as cosmotology (hairdressing), dental hygiene (training for dental nursing), technical training for industry, and so on. Athletics are prominent at most major universities, and students on athletic scholarships study while playing for the football, basketball or other teams.

Many students work their way through college. They enrol part time or full time, and simultaneously hold a job to support themselves. There are few financial awards available to American students, and those without parental support have to work or obtain a loan to be paid off after they graduate. Many male students are supported by working wives. Compared with Britain, for example, a high proportion of American students are married and have started their families, and the campus generally has accommodation for married students with children.

A peculiarly American feature of campus life is the system of fraternities (for men) and sororities (for women). To become a member of these social groups one must fulfil certain academic or personal requirements and go through an initiation ceremony. Fraternities form a personal unit in the impersonal university world, and can also bestow social status.

A university education is open to a much larger proportion of the Americans than in almost any other country. However, lack of financial resources can be a barrier, and the racial minorities and lower income groups are still under-represented. About a quarter of all black students attend largely segregated colleges, and these are often of lower quality and with less well qualified faculty.

University faculty are predominantly white males and almost half have doctoral degrees. Academic departments, headed by 'chairmen', are grouped into colleges run by deans and an administrative staff. Depending on the type of institution, the university will be headed by a President or Chancellor, who is the chief administrator, fund raiser and public relations officer. The operation of the institution or system of institutions is overseen by a Board of Regents, generally state or local political appointees whose predominantly business orientation will ensure that the universities continue to serve the interests of the economic system. The private institutions often have greater autonomy than the state colleges.

There is a distinct stratification of American colleges and a degree from the 'right' institution is worth far more than one from just any college. At the top of the prestige pyramid are the 'Ivy League' colleges such as Harvard, Yale, Princeton and Columbia, the leading science-oriented schools like the Massachusetts Institute of Technology, and the best of the public universities such as Berkeley (in the California state system). In the middle are most of the state colleges and the less prestigeful private institutions. At the bottom are the junior and community colleges, many of the southern black colleges, and some of those with a highly religious bias. The best offer an education comparable with that obtainable anywhere, and accompany it by helping to develop contacts in business and the professions, and by imprinting the style, manners and dress of the élite. The worst provide little more than a paper diploma.

SOME CURRENT ISSUES

A number of matters concerning education are major current political issues, and the subject of much public discussion. The most controversial is undoubtedly the 'bussing' of children as a means of achieving racial balance in schools. Until recently,

Black and White generally attended separate schools, but in 1954 the Supreme Court declared this unconstitutional. Since then there has been a gradual process of school desegregation, achieved largely by sending some white children to previously black schools by bus, and bussing black children in the other direction. This has led to outspoken and violent opposition from many white parents. They state a strong preference for the 'neighbourhood school', which because of segregated residential patterns would be predominantly a school of one race.

Another controversy centres on sex education in school, the introduction of which has been vigorously opposed by parents in some parts of the country. Similar passions are aroused by the question of prayers in public schools, ruled unconstitutional by the Supreme Court a few years ago. These issues both involve deeply held sets of values, with the closely intertwined puritan tradition, religious faith and patriotism conflicting with more liberal ideas.

Finance is a problem in the American educational system at all levels. There is currently a 'taxpayers' revolt', with an increasing number of educational bond issues defeated at the polls, and some school systems have had to close temporarily, due to lack of funds. Financial stringency also exists in higher education, with private colleges having difficulty keeping up with rising costs and state legislatures cutting their university budgets. These financial problems are in part a response to changing attitudes of the young, particularly on the college campuses. Students have become vocal advocates of peace, civil rights, poverty programmes and other liberal causes, which may be associated in the minds of the more conservative parents, taxpayers and prospective employers as unpatriotic or evidence of radical tendencies.

A particular concern among the young is that their education is irrelevant to their needs, and to the real needs of society at large. There is more emphasis on vocational courses than on a broad liberal education, and more training of technologists, lawyers and business executives than social workers and city planners. The solution of so many of the problems of contemporary

America appears to require not the conforming technocrats and administrators which the present education system produces, but more free-thinking humanists with a feel for the needs of ordinary people. Some of the young seem to sense this; their elders generally do not.

6

How They Get About

THE Americans are the most mobile people in the world. They move house frequently, they travel about a lot in the course of their daily lives, and they also go long distances on vacation or to visit relatives. Six million people live in 'mobile' homes, and although many of them are as permanently located as conventional houses they do in some way reflect the restlessness of a people accustomed to the idea of moving to where the opportunities are, in much the same way as the pioneers followed the advance of the frontier.

The nature of the economy requires high mobility of both personnel and goods. The distances separating cities now make air travel obligatory for many businessmen, while the covering of a salesman's territory can involve hours of automobile travel each day. Many thousands of agricultural workers live a migrant existence, following the seasons as they move from one harvest to another. Raw materials, components and finished products move around the country in volumes unequalled anywhere else, with the possible exception of north-west Europe.

American business and technology have responded to these needs for mobility with customary ingenuity and efficiency. There are the usual problems of traffic congestion, air pollution and noise associated with a modern transportation system, but for the most part people and commodities move about with ease. However, becoming thus highly mobile has involved some basic changes in the way people live, especially with respect to the growing dependence on the automobile.

TYPES OF TRANSPORT

The choice of transportation available to the private citizen in the United States is much the same as in any other advanced industrial nation. He is more likely than not to possess an automobile, he can use the airways if he can afford it, buses and trains are generally available along some if not all of the routes he may wish to travel, and there is also a limited amount of inland water transportation. However, compared with the western European, the American is more likely to use his car or go by air, and less likely to use a bus or a train. The recent rise of air travel has been mainly at the expense of the railroads and the bus lines, which now account for little more than 3 per cent of inter-city movement compared with almost 12 per cent twenty years ago.

The last twenty years have seen a substantial reduction in the proportional use of the railroads for the shipping of freight. The main beneficiary with respect to most products has been the motor carrier, but the figures are complicated by the increasing use of pipelines for the shipment of oil. Oil is the leading commodity in the United States today in terms of the volume of movement, and a complex system of pipelines now connects the oil and natural gas producing areas with the refineries and markets.

There is more movement of people and goods in some directions than others. The major manufacturing belt extending from New England into the mid-west is the region with the densest transport network, and the heaviest volumes of traffic. But there is an increasing connection coast to coast and with the south, as California and Florida continue their rapid growth. The most intensive movements occur within the cities, of course, with their daily flows of commuters in and out.

RAILROADS AND ROADS, WATERWAYS AND AIRWAYS

The development of the American railroad system was closely associated with the territorial expansion of the nation during the second half of the nineteenth century. The mileage of track reached a peak of over 260,000 in the 1920s, since when this has been reduced to the current figure of just over 200,000 miles. There are about 360 railroad operating companies, but the industry is dominated by a few large corporations. There are 29,000 locomotives in service, over 12,000 passenger cars, and almost $1\frac{1}{2}$ million freight wagons. The American railways carry about 300 million passengers each year, and account for almost 800 billion ton-miles of freight.

Only a small fraction of railroad revenues now come from passenger services. Long-distance passenger traffic is rapidly disappearing, as more businessmen take to the air and as families have taken to the automobile. For the businessman air travel has the great advantage of speed, and for the family on vacation the automobile, in association with the roadside motel, is a much more flexible means of getting about and has greater privacy and cleanliness than the railroad train. Thus the inter-city passenger business has steadily become less and less of an economic proposition for the railroads, and it has needed a government corporation (Amtrack) to continue services in the public interest. In contrast, the freight business has increased considerably during the past two decades, most of it in the relatively profitable long-haul business.

The loss of long-distance passenger traffic on the railroads has been paralleled by losses of intra-city traffic. Before the popularity of the automobile the railroads had a virtual monopoly of commuter traffic in many cities, but nationwide they account for only about 2 per cent of this today. There is currently much talk about the development of new mass-transit systems which would get commuters off the roads and back into the trains, but such systems will have to be extremely attractive to entice the average American away from his automobile.

A major reason for the demise of railroad passenger services, and the relatively faster growth of motor vehicle freight traffic when compared with the railroads, has been the improvement of the nation's road system. There are a total of 3,710,000 miles of roads in the United States, 550,000 of them municipal and the rest connecting the cities or serving rural areas. Whereas for a long time most of the roads outside the cities were gravel or 'dirt' roads, three-quarters of them are now surfaced.

The major road developments in recent years have been of two particular kinds—the system of Interstate Highways and the urban freeways. In 1944 a National System of Interstate and Defense Highways was proposed to improve the connections between the main metropolitan centres and industrial areas. The real start on this system came in the latter part of the 1950s, when the Federal-Aid Highway Act of 1956 provided for a federal contribution of 90 per cent to the states' 10 per cent for the construction of Interstate Highways. A network was planned, involving 41,000 miles of limited-access divided highways on which fairly high speeds could be maintained. More than 30,000 miles have now been completed, and the entire system should be finished by the middle of the 1970s—a remarkable feat of organisation and engineering.

The urban freeways are much the same as the Interstates, in that they are divided highways with restricted access. Their main purpose is to keep the rising flow of commuters moving in the morning and evening rush hours, and the busiest routes in the major cities can have five or six lanes in each direction. Where they intersect, or join the Interstates, there are elaborate 'clover-leaf' junctions with as many as four different road levels. No other sight so fully symbolises the mastery of the motor vehicle over the American urban environment.

Waterborne commerce, domestic and foreign, accounts for $1\frac{1}{2}$ billion short tons of goods shipped. Two-thirds of this is domestic. There are three major types of domestic waterborne commerce routes—the inland waterways (mainly rivers), the coastal sea routes, and the Great Lakes. The traditionally important Mississippi and Ohio River systems still provide thousands of miles of relatively cheap transportation, and their ports are as busy as most of those on the coast engaged in international trade. Focal points in the coastwise trade include the oil ports of the Texas Gulf Coast as well as some of the older ports on the Atlantic shore. The importance of the Great Lakes in the transportation system of the North American continent was greatly enhanced by the construction of the St Lawrence Seaway opened in 1959. This cost almost half a billion dollars, three-quarters of which was paid by Canada, and provides a continuous waterway of well over 2,000 miles which can take ocean-going vessels into the heart of the continent.

The past two decades have seen air travel become a familiar means by which increasing numbers of Americans get about. Almost every city and town has its connection with the national airways system, ranging from the unpaved airstrip of the small agricultural centre to the major international airports such as Kennedy in New York and O'Hare in Chicago, where a jet liner takes off every thirty seconds. To most businessmen, and even to a growing number of students at universities away from home, travel by air is as much a part of normal life as rail travel is to the average European. There is even a commuter service operating between New York and Washington where businessmen and government officials queue to get on the hourly flight, in much the same way as an Englishman will queue for his bus.

All this is possible because private business, supported by advances in aviation technology, has been quick to react to the growing need for greater personal mobility, and has itself stimulated further demand. By its very nature the airline business is the province of a few giants. There are only thirty-eight domestic air carriers in the country and most of those operate regional not nationwide services; only nine are international carriers.

There are over 11,000 airports in operation in the United States. Less than 1,000 have scheduled services, and more than half of them are private. The major air routes show a north-east to south-west axis, with most of the traffic connecting New York and other cities at the eastern end of the major manu-facturing belt with Los Angeles and San Francisco via Chicago and other large mid-western cities. To get on to these and other major domestic routes from the smaller cities usually requires at least one connecting flight. There are over 100,000 private planes in operation, and these are a favoured means by which senior businessmen, executives and rich families get about. In the more isolated parts of the country, in the west and in Alaska, for example, the light plane and the small unpaved runway form an essential part of the local transportation systems.

So popular and so necessary has air transportation become in contemporary America that it has almost outstripped even the ingenuity of American technology in finding solutions to some of the problems it brings. The air pollution and the noise arising from the use of increasing numbers of large jet planes are matters of growing concern. Another major difficulty is keeping up with airport construction, as the volume of traffic builds up. If there is a saturation point with respect to aviation, both in the air and on the ground, then the Americans are likely to find it first.

THE AUTOMOBILE IN AMERICAN LIFE

No single thing more epitomises the contemporary American way of life than the use of the automobile. There are now over 110 million motor vehicles registered in the United States—one for every two inhabitants, and more than double the figure of twenty years ago. Of these, 90 million are passenger cars. Less than one household in five is without a car; in the city suburbs it is one in ten, and a second car is considered almost a necessity to many middle-class families.

Sales of passenger cars fluctuate with the general level of prosperity, but during the 1960s it ranged from about 6 million to over 9 million annually. Each year the Americans scrap or 'junk' about 6 million cars—a greater number than the total motor vehicles in operation in all but the top half-dozen other advanced industrial nations. There are over 10 million automobiles in California alone.

The gradual reduction in the availability of public transport, particularly in the cities, makes the car a virtual necessity of life, without which the journey to work would be a nightmare, the transportation of children to school would be extremely difficult, and most shopping centres would be inaccessible.

For the carless family in the city, life is often confined to a particular neighbourhood, and for the inner-city poor many jobs (for example, on suburban construction sites) are placed beyond their reach simply by virtue of the impossibility of getting to them without a reliable car.

Designing ways in which Americans can go about their daily business without leaving their cars is a perpetual challenge to national ingenuity. The drive-in cinema is a well-known example of this, and the business strips along the main roads through the cities have a succession of drive-in restaurants. Drive-in windows are becoming increasingly common at banks (enabling customers to make a deposit or cash a cheque without going into the building), and also in dry cleaners, laundries, liquor stores, and a variety of other businesses. More unusual examples are the drive-in windows introduced at funeral homes in Atlanta and Detroit so that relatives and friends may view the deceased from the comfort of their cars. As the Atlanta mortician was quoted as saying, 'So many people want to come by and see the remains of a relative or friend, but they just don't have the time. This way they can drive by and just keep on going.' There are also a few drive-in churches, where people can park and plug in to a recorded service with piped music, on the way to the beach or family outing.

As well as its utilitarian function, the automobile has an important symbolic value. The size of cars and the variety of their designs make them conspicuous symbols of status and affluence, from which it is possible to make fairly accurate judgements about the owner's position in society. Some of the size is functional, for large cars are more comfortable on long drives and are useful in transporting half a dozen children to school as part of the 'car pool' through which families group together to solve this particular transportation problem. But some of it is purely decorative and carefully moulded to give the contemporary fashionable impression of speed, power or grandeur.

The automobile offers great scope for the American indulgence in gadgets. There are various optional extras which may be built into a new vehicle, and many of them are becoming so common as to be almost standard features. Of the cars produced in 1970, over 90 per cent had automatic transmission, 56 per cent power brakes, 81 per cent power steering, 17 per cent power windows (ie operated by pressing a knob), and 61 per cent air conditioning. Despite all these refinements American cars are not expensive when related to wage levels. The average new car in 1970 cost only just over $3,000, or less than one-third of the income of the average family. One reason why they are so cheap is that they are not made to last (ie they have 'built-in obsolescence'), either in the mechanical sense or in terms of design. In the autumn of each year the manufacturer brings out his new designs, and the proud owner of last year's model is immediately under pressure to 'trade in' and buy a new one.

Cars are important masculinity symbols in the United States. Sex appeal figures prominently in advertising, particularly in the case of sports models. Names such as the Charger, Mustang, Cougar and Thunderbird are not chosen lightly by the manufacturers; they evoke a proper impression of aggressive manliness, and allow the purchaser some means of identifying with an image of himself which he is unlikely to be able to play out in his normal daily life.

The purchase of an automobile also has the incidental attraction of allowing the individual to exercise another personal quality much admired in the American male—skill in financial negotiation. Because the price actually paid for a new car will be substantially less than the price supposedly recommended by the manufacturer, and because it is complicated by the cost of the extras and by the trade-in value of the old car, the figure is subject to discussion, and the transaction leaves most buyers feeling that their bargaining skills have enabled them to get 'a good deal'. The parallel with horse trading in the frontier days is striking.

Owning and operating a car are likely to cost something like one-tenth of the average family's annual income of $10,000. The estimated cost of running a four-door sedan costing about $3,400 for ten years was calculated to be $11,890 in 1970. This works out at almost eleven cents per mile driven.

The industries concerned with providing the American with his automobile and keeping it running make up a substantial share of the national economy. The three largest single manufacturing industries in the United States are motor vehicle production, petroleum refining, and the making of motor vehicle parts and accessories, and together their total value of shipments annually comes to over $60 billion. To this must be added the large segment of the steel and rubber industries supplying the auto manufacturers, and the multi-billion dollar auto-insurance industry. Then there are the thousands of service stations and repair shops kept going by high gasoline consumption of the powerful engines in American cars, and the large amount of repair work required as a result of the slightest impact in a collision.

At the hub of this closely interrelated automobile industrial complex is General Motors, the world's largest industrial firm. General Motors, together with the other automobile manufacturers, the giant oil corporations, and other auto-related industries, have the capacity to exercise considerable influence on both private and public expenditure in the United States. This helps to explain the predominance of the automobile in American life. The fact that Americans are prepared to spend so much simply on getting about by car, particularly when compared with their reluctance to tax themselves to pay for education and other public services, can be attributed at least in part to the power of media advertising which stresses the importance of car ownership.

The orientation of American society towards the automobile is a source of great personal convenience, but it also exacts a price. Currently about 55,000 people are killed on the roads each year (more than all the US soldiers lost in Vietnam), and the total road deaths in the 1960s approached half a million. Exhaust fumes are polluting the air of most major cities, and metropolitan areas throughout the land have been re-designed, and neighbourhoods torn down, so that people in cars can get about more easily. If the price of the motorised society is high it is a price the Americans seem prepared to pay, such is their dedication to the automobile.

7

How They Amuse Themselves

AFFLUENCE brings with it the possibility of spending more time in leisure pursuits. It also brings greater capacity to purchase amusement, and broadens the range of recreational and creative outlets available. The Americans amuse themselves in a wide variety of ways. For many, the traditional pleasures of social life dominate leisure time—playing at home or with school friends for children, dating and peer-group activities for teenagers and young adults, and dinner parties with friends or a family get-together for the more mature. But many amusements are big business, and call for a substantial share of individual and family expenditure.

During the 1960s personal spending on recreation doubled. Although this does not include all forms of amusement, the allocation of expenditure on different types of recreation gives some idea of the way the Americans express their preferences:

Type of Product or Service	$m spent 1969
Books, magazines, newspapers, etc	7,004
Non-durable toys and sports supplies	5,213
Wheel goods, durable toys, sports equipment, boats, etc	4,219
Radio and TV receivers, records and musical instruments	8,085
Radio and TV repair	1,266
Garden supplies	1,361
Admission to cinemas, theatres, spectator sports, etc	2,260

Type of Product or Service	$m spent 1969
Clubs and fraternal organisations	1,108
Commercial participant amusements	1,719
Others, including betting, photography, collecting, etc	4,070
Total recreational expenditures	36,305

This chapter concentrates on the leading forms of organised amusement which require some expenditure on the part of the participants.

COMMUNICATION AND THE MASS MEDIA

For many Americans the mass communication media provide the most accessible and common forms of amusement. The ownership of television is now almost universal, and in most parts of the country there is continuous broadcasting on a choice of channels from perhaps 6.00 am to 2.00 am the following morning. There are almost 700 commercial television broadcasting stations, most of them mainly relaying the programmes of the three national networks of CBS (Columbia Broadcasting System), ABC (Associated Broadcasting Corporation) and NBC (National Broadcasting Corporation). These programmes are commercially sponsored, and interspersed with advertising messages which occupy something like one-fifth of air time. In addition there is the Public Broadcasting System incorporating National Educational Television (locally relayed by about 150 stations), which caters mainly to educated minority interests.

It was recently estimated that by the end of their lives today's children will have spent the equivalent of ten years watching television. By conventional criteria, this is not likely to have been an elevating experience. In children's television the traditional emphasis is on cartoons, often with a large content of violence, though the past couple of years have seen more emphasis on

education. Many children's programmes have a strong sales
pitch (anything from toys to a brand of bread) which is often
not easy to distinguish from the entertainment content. For
adults daytime television comprises a series of romantic sagas
known as 'soap operas', while in the evenings the emphasis is
on variety shows, crime series, and so on. As the prime function
of the programmes is to sell the sponsor's product, the networks
show what most people will watch, and assiduously avoid controversial matter or anything likely to offend the viewer. The
main exceptions to the generally mediocre quality of American
television are sports and news programmes. The former are
done with great expertise. The latter are of high quality by
any standards, with the three major networks assembling news-
casters and commentators with national reputations for objectivity and accuracy of reporting (except in the eyes of conserva-
tives who see them as too liberal in philosophy).

There are over 5,000 radio stations in the United States. Their
main function is to relay advertisements and the occasional few
minutes of news, interspersed with popular music. Except in
cities, and in university towns with a radio station on campus,
it is rare to hear discussions of current affairs or classical music
on the radio.

Most American families take a daily and Sunday newspaper.
These are generally larger than in Europe, partly because of
the high advertising content; in 1970 the average number of
pages per issue for dailies was 50, and for Sundays over 150. The
size of the Sunday edition of the *New York Times* is remarkable,
for it weighs about seven pounds, runs to perhaps 400 pages,
and costs the city ten cents a copy to dispose of as garbage.
There are no national newspapers, but many of the local and
city papers belong to large national combines like the Hearst
Corporation, the New York Times, and the Washington Post
Company. There are 1,800 daily papers published across the
country, and nine out of ten have a monopoly in their area of
circulation.

Some of the functions of national newspapers are performed
by the leading city papers, especially the *New York Times* and

the *Washington Post*, which can be obtained nationwide. In addition there are a number of news weeklies which have large national circulation, the best known being *Time* and *Newsweek*. There are also large sales of other periodicals appealing to special professional, technical and political groups. Subscription to periodicals is generally by mail, as the cost this way is only a fraction of what it is on the news-stands or in the shops.

Freedom to use the airways and the press to express opinions without official retribution is a fiercely protected American right. The major television networks operate some *de facto* censorship, in that they have on occasions required the exclusion of politically sensitive matter disliked by the sponsoring business interests. There is also some current concern at the extent to which the government may be prepared to try to influence the media to play down news critical of the Administration. But in general news and ideas flow freely and easily, and Americans can usually hear and read what they want to.

CINEMAS AND THE PERFORMING ARTS

A visit to the cinema is still one of the most common forms of amusement, despite a falling off of attendance with the advent of television. There are about 14,000 motion picture theatres in operation today (about 4,000 of them drive-ins), compared with 19,000 in 1950. But the nature of the industry is changing, and recent studio closures accompanied by the success of some movies made on very small budgets suggest that the days of the Hollywood extravaganzas and superstars may be coming to an end.

The theatre in America largely consists of Broadway in New York. The number of shows averaged about eighty a year throughout the 1960s, but attendance has not expanded in proportion to the population and economic growth. The Broadway theatre reached its peak some time ago, probably in the 1920s, and though a few 'hits' still make great profits the theatre as a whole is in financial difficulties. The post-war growth of the off-

Broadway theatre seems to have slowed down in recent years; there are now more shows off than on Broadway, but attendance is only about a million a year compared with 7 million on Broadway.

There are about thirty entirely professional symphony orchestras, playing seasons ranging from twenty-two to fifty-two weeks a year. The best of them are among the leading orchestras in the world. In addition there are other semi-professional metropolitan orchestras, and enough others in smaller communities and in colleges to give the nation over 1,440 symphony orchestras altogether. The major orchestras attract about 9 million concert-goers each year.

The only major opera companies are in New York, Chicago and San Francisco, but there are another forty or so professional and semi-professional groups. Annual attendance is about 2 million. Ballet probably attracts less than a million spectators each year. Like opera, it is available only in the largest cities and occasionally in college towns.

In general, public attendance at and support of the performing arts appears to be growing at a slower rate than expenditures on science and education, for example. One obvious reason is the refinement and the general availability of substitutes such as records. American industry and technology have been able to provide these substitutes relatively cheaply, while the price of attending live performances has risen with the growing cost of running organisations like a major orchestra.

CLUBS AND OTHER ORGANISATIONS

There are thousands of clubs and other organised bodies which provide the Americans with a setting for social interaction and other forms of amusement. The various common interests on which these are based include trade, business, culture, public affairs, nationality or ethnicity, patriotism, hobbies, religion, sport and charity.

For children the Boy Scouts and Girl Guides are available.

But they do not have a large following, as most participatory group activity is associated with school and sport. In the inner cities some attempts have been made to assist disadvantaged children through clubs of various kinds.

For men there are a variety of business, professional and fraternal organisations. Local businessmen belong to the Rotary or a masonic temple or 'shrine'. Leading fraternal associations include the Elks, the Lions and the Moose, which have lodges in most communities. Most of the fraternal associations are exclusively for Whites, and are bastions of traditional values. The American Legion and the Veterans of Foreign Wars are leading patriotic organisations.

Clubs for women range from associations related to occupation (such as legal secretaries or dental auxiliaries), and from religious and cultural groups, to 'Greek letter' sororities engaged in gossip or good works. As an illustration of the variety, a city of 80,000 people in which these authors lived has over seventy different active women's clubs.

Clubs not only help to fill time and structure social activity, but also provide an arena for status seeking. Membership of a particular country club may be regarded as an important social distinction, and also a practical advantage in conducting business. There may be subtle differences between women's clubs, on the basis of the social status attached to membership. Voluntary associations also perform activist and watchdog functions with respect to civil rights and liberties, where the official local government structure may be reluctant to investigate or take action.

COMPETITIVE SPORT

Sports of various kind offer the Americans both the opportunity to compete and a formal channel for the assertive behaviour admired in the American male. The Americans participate and spectate in large numbers. The major competitive team sports are big business, not only in the professional leagues, but also on the college circuits from which the professional clubs recruit their players. College stars can become instant millionaires, with salaries of over $100,000 a year for the top professional players added to large signing-on fees. The franchises through which the leagues who run the major professional sports sanction the existence of a team in a particular city change hands for millions of dollars, and their possession is generally a lucrative business. Televised professional sport is closely associated with the advertising campaigns of major manufacturing industries, appealing to the male market with the latest innovations in shaving technology as well as automobiles and beer.

In the eyes of the outside world baseball is the most 'American' of the nation's sports. The twenty or so major-league clubs attract about 30 million spectators annually, to which may be added 10 million who watch the minor leagues. The basic objective in baseball is very simple—for a series of batters to hit a ball thrown by the pitcher of the other team far enough to enable them to run round a square comprising four bases. A run can be earned in stages, or in one blow by hitting a 'home run' into the crowd. The pitcher rather than the batter is the real star in baseball, and much of the attention is focused on his performance. The baseball season is climaxed by the World Series, during which over a quarter of a million people watch games between the winners of each of the two major leagues to decide the championship of America, ie the world.

In recent years baseball has declined somewhat in its popularity compared with football. College football is traditionally one of the favourite spectator sports, and the leading colleges run their teams as slick business operations. They can regularly fill stadiums with 60,000 or more spectators, and the total college football audience is as large as for major-league baseball. During the post-war era there has been a rapidly growing interest in professional football, which now attracts 10 million people a year compared with only one-fifth of this twenty years ago, as well as television audiences of millions for each game broadcast. Like the major-league baseball clubs, the professional football clubs generally operate in the larger cities.

The Americans have stamped their own distinctive character

on the game of football. American football is played with an oval ball, which a team will attempt to advance up the field either by a player running with it or by the 'quarter-back' who leads the offence throwing a forward overarm pass to be caught by a 'receiver' upfield. But on to this basic strategy is built a structure of incredible complexity. There are an almost infinite variety of different moves or 'plays' which a team can try, and they are carefully planned in advance and discussed on the field in the 'huddle' which precedes each individual play. Every activity of the player is subject to measurement—the number of tackles, the number of completed passes, the number of yards gained and so on, and a record is kept of each player's average yards gained per carry, average length of punt, etc. Just as in baseball players who make a conspicuous mistake are charged with an 'error', so in football to drop the ball is officially to 'fumble'. It is almost as though two separate games are being played—one tallied by the points scored by 'touchdowns' (like tries in Rugby football), conversions and 'field goals' (place kicks), and the other by the individual and team statistics.

There is a great deal of symbolism in American football. The players wear elaborate padding and helmets, which create the impression of supermen with unusually broad shoulders—an idealised male form. They struggle to control territory, by a combination of brute strength and guile. The territory they fight for is increasingly becoming artificial turf—an expensive large green rug which allows them to play out their carefully contrived conflict without slipping in the mud. The major college football game is the closest thing to a tribal ritual to be seen in America outside the Indian Reservations, as the crowds are urged on to wild crescendoes of enthusiasm by bright-costumed cheer-leaders to the accompaniment of the college band, while their heroes do battle on the field.

Basketball is similar to football in that it has a large college following and a growing professional league. Together they attract about 20 million spectators each year.

Tenpin bowling is another distinctively American sporting activity. It is mainly amateur, with the organised leagues having over 7 million members. Most towns and cities have bowling alleys, many of which serve the subsidiary function of social centres, particularly for blue-collar workers and their families. Billiard halls are also gathering places for men across the land. Boxing and wrestling have considerable followings, but the largest strictly spectator sport by a wide margin is horse racing with about 70 million a year. Golf is a popular middle-class male activity, with an estimated 10 million participants.

OUTDOOR RECREATION

No other country on earth offers a greater range of opportunities for outdoor recreation. In winter skiing is available within fairly easy access of the major population concentrations in the north-east and on the west coast, as well as at resorts in the Rockies. The sea and the lakes offer boating and water skiing to the increasing number of Americans with the money to indulge in these activities. And for those who like to soak up the sun and swim there are hundreds of miles of beaches.

A less actively participant type of outdoor recreation is viewing the scenic splendour of the nation. This is a common form of vacation, and can be done in a variety of ways. At the one extreme is the well-off family who tour in their air-conditioned Cadillac or Lincoln Continental, staying at the best hotels and motels, or pulling a luxury Airstream trailer. At the other are the less affluent and the young, travelling in a Volkswagen or older car and using camp-sites. In between is the average American family, with a two-year-old station waggon or sedan and using the cheaper chain and small private motels.

The National Parks are a major attraction to the motorised vacationer. These cover almost 30 million acres, and include areas of outstanding natural beauty and also National Monuments, historic sites, and military historical areas. They are carefully protected by the National Parks Service, who provide information centres and a staff of rangers to assist the visitor. Although there are trails which the hardy can follow into the wilderness, most of the scenery in the National Parks can be viewed from the automobile. Accommodation, food and other services within the parks are provided by private business 'concessions' regulated by the National Parks Service. In almost all cases, visits to the National Parks are a rewarding experience, though of those most widely known Yosemite has become very crowded during recent years and Yellowstone has poor food and accommodation. The National Parks system is probably the world's most successful large-scale programme of nature conservation and recreational development, undertaken with a sensitive understanding of the proper balance between the protection and use of the areas concerned. The number of visitors annually now approaches 200 million, almost four times the number twenty years ago, and there is growing concern that the more popular parks may have to restrict vehicular access in some way if they are not to become severely overcrowded.

In addition to the National Parks there are various kinds of State Parks. These are similar to the National Parks, in that they include historic sites and areas of special natural beauty. They tend to be more accessible than the National Parks, most of which are in the west, and attract more than twice the number of visitors. Some of them have overnight accommodation in cabins or hotels, and in 1970 there were 50 million overnight visitors to State Parks throughout the nation compared with 16 million at the National Parks. These parks generally provide camping facilities and areas where families can enjoy a 'cookout'.

HUNTING AND SHOOTING

For many Americans, outdoor recreation means hunting of some kind. There are about 30 million fishing licences issued annually, and 20 million for hunting with guns. Game of various types is available in almost all of rural America, and hunting is a popular activity which provides an outlet for the frontiersman lurking in the American character.

Hunting is a way in which society sanctions the traditional

reverence and respect for guns. Americans derive great satisfaction from possessing and handling guns, and from using them to shoot things. It is estimated that over 90 million firearms are privately owned in America, or almost one for every two citizens—by far the highest guns to population ratio in the world. Most of these are probably sporting guns, or rifles, but there may be 25 million handguns or pistols among them.

The possession of guns in America has an obvious historical precedent. It recalls the 'winning of the West', and is part of a national tendency to legitimise violent solutions to personal conflict. A leading paediatrician recently estimated that by the time an average American child is eleven he can expect to have seen 18,000 people killed on television. Whether this breeds violence is difficult to demonstrate, but it certainly engenders a familiarity with the use of guns to resolve conflict. Just as the hunter will shoot his quarry, so a policeman may fire at a fleeing suspect and a householder at an intruder without a second thought.

Some recent events have led to a growing questioning of the constitutional right of Americans to 'keep and bear arms'. These include the shooting of President Kennedy, two Presidential contenders (Robert Kennedy and George Wallace), and a leading national spokesman for black civil rights (Martin Luther King), as well as an annual rate of about 10,000 killings and over 70,000 aggravated assaults by firearms. Some politicians are advocating legislation which would control the ownership of guns, or at least require their registration. But this faces vigorous opposition from the hunters and from the strong National Rifle Association lobby in Washington who look after the interests of the rifle manufacturing industry. The perennial Communist plot is invoked and the NRA distribute auto bumper stickers reading: 'If guns are outlawed, only outlaws will have guns.' The anguish over the murder of national leaders soon evaporates, and it may take a few more before the Americans will willingly control the ownership and use of this major instrument of personal amusement and protection.

8

The Problems They Face

No account of how the Americans live and work would be complete without some discussion of their major problems. These are matters of great importance, for how they are resolved will help to determine the future character of national life in this era of rapid change, and they occupy much current public attention with frequent exposure on the news media. Some of these problems have been introduced already. This chapter brings them together, with a few suggestions as to how they relate to one another and to certain basic facts of American life.

POVERTY AND SOCIAL DEPRIVATION

The existence of a substantial minority of poor people amidst the affluence of contemporary America has been described as one of the nation's enduring paradoxes. It has always had its poor, of course, but not until the beginning of the 1960s did they begin to attract real public attention and concern. The publication of Michael Harrington's book *The Other America* in 1962 was particularly influential, with its claim that one American in five lived in poverty, many of them hidden from view in the valleys of Appalachia and the city ghettos—an 'invisible land' to most of the population. These revelations, which were confirmed by various government inquiries, led to the 'War on Poverty' of the Johnson Administration, under which programmes to assist the poor were initiated. By the end of the decade the number of people officially classified as poor had been reduced by about 15 million from a total of 40 million in 1960.

But despite this progress the poor are still there in substantial numbers. The official poverty level established by calculating the income needed to meet basic living expenses was set at just under $4,000 for a non-farm family of four in mid-1971. By this criterion there were 25,500,000 people living in poverty (over 12 per cent of the total population) according to the US Bureau of the Census, to which may be added a further 10 million with incomes not much over the poverty level.

Poverty in America is a highly selective condition, affecting some segments of the population to a much greater extent than others. At the beginning of the 1970s almost 40 per cent of families headed by a woman were in poverty, compared with only 8 per cent of those with male heads. Almost 30 per cent of all non-white families are poor, compared with only 8 per cent of white families. Of black families headed by someone with less than eight years of schooling, 40 per cent are poor, compared with 21 per cent of white families with heads in the same educational category. Farm dwellers are twice as likely to be poor as non-farm dwellers.

Poverty is also geographhlicaly selective. There is a clear regional concentration, with almost 15 per cent of all families in the South in poverty in 1971 (37·5 for non-whites) compared with 8·9 per cent in the West, 8 per cent in the North Central Region, and 7 per cent in the North East. Although a higher proportion of rural than urban families are poor, about two-thirds of those in poverty live in urban areas.

Poverty, in the sense of inadequate income, is generally accompanied by other conditions of social deprivation. These include poor housing and general environmental quality, hunger and malnutrition, high death-rates and incidence of various illnesses, and low-quality social services. All this adds up to what is sometimes described as 'the culture of poverty'. Children born to poor parents start off life with a disadvantage they may never overcome. Their poor diets in infancy may impair their mental faculties, even before they enter the highly inadequate schools. They grow up in a home where the father, if he is still there, is a conspicuous failure as a provider for his family, and (in the city) in a neighbourhood rife with crime, prostitution, drug addiction, and other forms of social deviance. They enter adult life quite unequipped for the demands of the highly competitive contemporary industrial/technological society, drift from one poorly paid job to another, and more often than not never break out of the cycle of poverty into which they were born.

How is it that conditions such as these can still afflict one in ten of the people of the most affluent nation on earth? How is it that a society with such energy and technical expertise has not committed its great resources to the establishment of effective programmes to combat poverty and other forms of deprivation? The reasons lie somewhere in a set of national attitudes which tend to consider the poor as inadequate individuals living on welfare handouts provided by the hard-earned tax dollars of others, rather than as victims of external circumstances over which they have little if any personal control. These attitudes influence both the legislators who design and vote social programmes into law, and some of the public officials who administer them.

Thus present policies are not really designed to come to grips with the basic causes of poverty. They are not concerned with the operation of the economic system which at present denies work to 5 million unemployed while many millions of others are in low-wage industries, and which has steadily concentrated more and more of the nation's resources into the hands of the rich. They are not concerned with offering the poor a real alternative to the environment of the slums, unless they can pull themselves up by their own bootstraps. Anything approaching the kind of welfare state familiar to many Europeans would be decried as Socialism, and seen as a threat to the prevailing 'free-enterprise' system and to the ethic of individual initiative which supports it. So all that existing programmes can do is to provide very limited help, at the same time exacting a price in terms of the loss of human dignity associated with being 'on 'welfare'. And even these meagre offerings are denied to many people in need, because of the way in which programmes are administered.

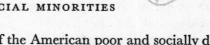

THE RACIAL MINORITIES

Although the majority of the American poor and socially deprived are white, the proportional incidence of these conditions is highest among the racial minorities. These include chiefly the Blacks, the Indians, and Spanish-speaking Americans.

The problems of the American Negroes, or Blacks, are particularly difficult. They make up about 12 per cent of the nation's population, but more than a century after the abolition of slavery following the war between the states most of the Blacks have yet to become full citizens of the United States in the sense of participating in American life as equals. Emancipation changed the conditions of black farm workers in the South relatively little, and those who moved north found life little better. Not until the 1950s did Blacks in significant numbers gain the confidence to question and actively oppose their traditional exclusion from schools, hotels, restaurants, drug-store lunch counters and voting booths, hitherto reserved for the Whites. The justice of their claims for equality and integration was recognised by enough white middle-class liberals to create a political climate in which some action could be taken. This began with the Supreme Court school desegregation decision, and culminated in the Civil Rights Act of 1964, which made various forms of racial discrimination illegal.

Despite considerable progress made during the past two decades, the Blacks are still worse off than white Americans in practically every sphere of national life. Blacks suffer from low incomes, poor housing, ill health, malnutrition, low education, high crime and so on, to a markedly greater extent than the population at large. They own only about 1 per cent of all businesses, they tend to hold the more menial and unskilled jobs, and they are prevented from advancing in some industries by the discriminatory practices of labour unions. They are poorly represented in the universities, both in the student bodies and on the faculties. They are under-represented in professions such as medicine and the law, they occupy very few senior administrative positions, and they have virtually no representation at all in the major sources of economic power such as banking and the boardrooms of giant industrial corporations. There are only about a dozen black congressmen, and Blacks account for few important elected officials locally even in their own communities, where school boards and city councils are often controlled by the white minority. Only on the welfare rolls and in the Vietnam dead are the Blacks conspicuously over-represented when compared with their share of the national population.

In absolute terms, the social and economic conditions of the black family have improved in some respects in recent years, though the gap separating them from the Whites has not narrowed to any significant degree. In some ways they may be worse off; for example, the rising figures for illegitimacy and fatherless families indicate a real threat to the existence of the family unit in some urban black communities. Overt racial discrimination is now hard to find, even in the South, but Blacks are still excluded from schools, jobs and welfare programmes by more subtle means. The growing frustration of Blacks over the difference between expectation and reality is expressing itself in some new ways, for example in the city riots of the late 1960s and in the emergence of the Black Power movement with its militant Black Panther party.

The growing militancy of the Blacks during the last few years has been accompanied by a search for the racial identity denied to them for so long in the white-dominated society. Rather than being ashamed of their colour and physical characteristics, the young now emphasise these with their bushy 'Afro' or 'natural' hair styles and the slogan 'Black is Beautiful'. Some call themselves Afro-Americans and even wear African-style clothing. Black studies programmes have been initiated at many colleges, and there is a growing interest in African history and culture. At the extreme, these feelings of black identity are expressed in a total rejection of white society and in a desire to 'do their own thing' in their own way in their own communities or in a black nation.

Some of the worst poverty in America is on the Indian Reservations. As the frontier of white settlement moved steadily westwards during the nineteenth century, the Indians were driven from their homelands and gradually relegated to the reservations. The land they were permitted to occupy in the end was that for which the Whites had no real use—generally infertile land in the arid basins and plains of the Dakotas and the south-west. Here most of today's Indians who have not migrated to the cities can do little more than eke out a bare subsistence from the land, supplemented in places by producing their traditional crafts for tourists. As many as three-quarters of all reservation Indian families probably have incomes below the poverty level. The colourful tepees and feathers of the past have been replaced by crude wooden shacks and faded blue jeans, and the horse is giving way to the second-hand car or pick-up truck. About 40 per cent of rural farm-dwelling Indians have less than five years' schooling; for rural non-farm Indians and those in urban areas the proportions are 32 per cent and 15 per cent respectively. More than half the Indian children have to leave home to go to school, and this tends to break up normal family life. Health conditions are low, and the average Indian lives about twenty years less than is normal for Americans. Alcoholism is a problem on some reservations and suicide rates are high.

Far from helping the Indians to cope with some of these problems, the government, through the Department of Indian Affairs, has tended to perpetuate them. The emphasis in the Indian schools is on standard academic subjects designed to help them assimilate into the wider framework of American life, with little attention paid to Indian language and culture. Thus the Indians have tended to lose some of their distinctive identity, and hence an important source of self-respect. The current reaction to this is similar to that of the young Blacks, with demands for more say in their own affairs and for the

K

right to stay out of the 'melting pot' of American cultural homogenisation and be themselves.

There are two main groups of Spanish-speaking Americans. One is the Puerto Ricans and others attracted to New York and a few other north-eastern cities during the last two decades. The other, and by far the more numerous, consists of about 5 million Mexican immigrants or descendants of immigrants drawn to the south-west by employment prospects in the growing industrial and agricultural economy. Both the Puerto Ricans and the 'Chicanos' occupy low positions on the socio-economic ladder, and find the climb up extremely difficult. For example, about four out of five Mexican-Americans work in low status blue-collar, service and farm labouring jobs, and about twice as many live in poverty as in the American population at large. Access to better-paying jobs for such people is hampered by poor education, and in the case of the more recent immigrant by a language problem. Living conditions for the Mexican-American farm labourer in California can be severe, but the 'barrios' of the cities such as Los Angeles to which some of them move offer only the alternatives of the slums.

As well as occupying lowly social and economic status, most members of the racial minority groups are discriminated against in various ways. They claim, with some justification, that they are harassed by the police, and that some courts deal with them more harshly than they would with Whites. They are denied some employment opportunities open to Whites with no better qualifications. And what is perhaps most serious, their children are often denied the special educational treatment which they need to break out of the cycle of poverty.

Despite a growing public awareness of the plight of the racial minorities, and rhetorical expressions of sympathy on the part of politicians and administrators, America is a long way from adequately dealing with the problem. Racial prejudice, particularly towards Blacks, is a deep-seated trait of many white Americans, which can still erupt into extreme hatred among the working class who feel a threat to their economic and social status. In order to take their rightful place in American society the minority groups need more than equal-opportunity laws and public expressions of concern. They need substantial compensatory programmes of remedial education and job training, which will cost large sums of money. They need to be able to see enough real opportunities for economic advancement to revive the motivation and the will to work which many Blacks and others appear to have lost. And they need the help of sympathetic public officials responsive to human needs in place of the cold bureaucrats with which they so often have to deal. At present it seems doubtful whether the Americans at large are yet prepared to go this far, in order to pull the racial minorities up into the mainstream of national life, and thus into a position to compete for the benefits of the affluent society.

THE CITIES

The problems of poverty and social deprivation, and of the racial minorities, are now largely concentrated in the major cities. They have always had their ghettos of poor people, where successive waves of foreign immigrants were first absorbed. But the past two decades have seen a new kind of immigration, with the massive influx of Blacks from the South. Displaced by mechanisation in agriculture, and seeking escape from the racial repression of the South, over 2 million poor and largely unskilled Blacks have moved to the cities of the north. The prospects of work were one attraction, but another has been the relatively high level of the welfare payments. Most major cities now have large impoverished black ghettos, and in some, including Washington DC, Blacks now comprise a majority of the population.

It is in the city ghettos that the social problems are concentrated. Along with high unemployment, low incomes and material poverty are the associated conditions of broken homes, low educational achievement, high infant mortality, high tuberculosis and other death-rates, high crime levels, and high incidence of alcoholism and drug abuse. The growing drug problem is a matter of current concern, with an estimated 100,000 to 200,000 heroin addicts in New York City and over 30,000 in Washington DC. The sale of narcotics is a lucrative part of the business of organised crime in the cities. As addicts steal or become prostitutes to support their habit, they set in motion chains of criminal activity which may cost half a billion dollars a year in Washington DC, and well over a billion in New York City.

The enormity of the problems of the city slums in the United States is hard to grasp. So far, the main attempt to improve matters has comprised tearing down the slums and building subsidised public housing projects. But because the basic causes of poverty have remained largely untouched, life in the 'projects' is often little better than in the slums. Public housing has tended to be designed and located with little regard to real human needs, and whatever feeling of community may have existed in the old neighbourhoods is soon lost in anonymous concrete blocks of flats. With the failure of this kind of urban renewal to solve social problems, the emphasis has now shifted to environmental rehabilitation, as in the Model Cities programme.

Urban poverty and social problems are by no means confined to the black ghettos. Every city has large areas where white blue-collar workers live, earning $5,000 to $10,000 a year and struggling to keep up with the rapidly rising cost of food, medical care, and taxes to support education and other local services. With their neighbourhoods deteriorating in the path of the growing ghetto, yet unable to afford to move to the better suburbs, these are the people who feel most threatened by the Blacks. These are the working-class 'ethnics' of predominantly Irish, Polish and central and eastern European descent. Unwilling to recognise the inadequacies of their lives, and often too proud to accept welfare, they may be worse off and suffer from poorer public services than some of the ghetto Blacks.

With the growing number of welfare cases to support, and with the rising cost of public services, many major American cities are in a serious financial position. Some have had to curtail services, and lay off public employees. As white-collar workers and businesses move out of the city limits into the suburbs the city's tax base is reduced, and the problems simply get worse. There are now serious questions as to whether New York and other large cities can continue to function effectively with their existing governmental and tax structures, without massive federal revenue support.

In the suburbs the picture is different. The affluent middle class who generally make their money in the city pay their taxes to their own community, thus supporting the good-quality education and other services which the inner-city residents lack. By the use of zoning laws requiring low-density housing development, and by simple racial discrimination, the suburban communities are generally able to keep out the poor and the Blacks, and resist attempts to build public housing. The relocation of slum dwellers in new estates on the edge of the city has proved to be almost impossible. Thus the major American city is becoming geographically segregated along racial and social class lines, with the poor Blacks in the centre, the affluent Whites on the fringe, and the white proletariat often between them.

These social problems are only part of what is often referred to as the 'crisis' in the cities. Other problems include the decreasing efficiency of some public services including garbage collection and public transportation, the fragmentation of metropolitan government into large numbers of independent political units, the lack of co-ordination in city and regional planning, and the quality of the physical environment. In general, the American city is operated in the interests of business and the owners of land and capital. Thus the stringent control of the development of land familiar in many European countries is viewed as an infringement of economic freedom in the United States. The freedom of the individual to realise the 'highest and best use' of his land usually transcends any conflicting interests of the public at large, and the kind of imaginative and creative city planning which requires public co-ordination is thus relatively rare. Suburbs sprawl into the countryside, and the industrial and commercial districts are characterised by an

ugliness almost unrelieved by any buildings of architectural
distinction. There are exceptions, of course, such as the prestige
offices of some of the major corporations. And the United States
has two privately developed new towns (Columbia in Maryland
and Reston in Virginia) which compare favourably with any
in Europe. But serious city and regional planning is still some
way away in most parts of the country and until the Americans
are prepared to accept more restrictions on the freedom to
develop land how they please the cities are likely to continue
their present unregulated and chaotic outward expansion and
inner deterioration.

THE 'DEMOCRATIC' SYSTEM

American government has so far been rather unresponsive to
the problems of the cities and to the needs of the poor and
socially deprived people. The social welfare system is incom-
plete and lacks co-ordination, and it is failing to break people
out of the cycle of poverty and dependence. City governments
are increasingly unable to cope with their mounting problems,
and federal involvement is still largely experimental. The proportion of national resources, energy and ingenuity devoted to
tackling these problems is small when compared with what is
spent on defence and prestige technology like space exploration
and on the production of goods and services for the affluent
majority.

The reasons for this ultimately trace back to societal values,
and the national priorities resting on them. But some relate
more directly to imperfections in the democratic system, which
have led to the under-representation of some interests and have
given great political influence to others. Until very recently
most Blacks in the South were denied the vote by literacy tests
and by threats of economic sanction and physical brutality.
Many are still not registered to vote and the same applies to
the Spanish-speaking immigrants. Even when they have the
vote, the socially deprived and the racial minorities often have

no candidate sympathetic to their plight or of their own people. In addition, the southern rural conservative control of so many congressional committees means that the interests of the poor and of the major metropolitan areas tend to be under-represented in national government.

In contrast, government generally seems to be extremely responsive to the requirements of the rich and of the big business interests. The taxation system has numerous 'loopholes' which enable some of the rich to avoid paying and which give some industries such as oil a position of privilege. Government agencies are often reluctant to regulate firmly the activities of business. And many social programmes could have been financed out of the billions of federal dollars spent on public works projects and abortive weapons systems which have benefited the contractors far more than the American people at large.

That such a differential response to the needs of different segments of society should exist is not surprising, in the light of the way in which American democracy operates. Reference has already been made in Chapter 2 to the power of lobbies and vested business interests to influence legislation, and to the growing problem of election financing. To stand for a major elected public office, a candidate must now either be a multi-millionaire or obtain the backing of other wealthy individuals or corporations. If the former is the case, he is unlikely to be closely in touch with the feelings of the poor and socially deprived, though there have been exceptions such as the Kennedy brothers. If the latter, then there is a danger that the candidate will become the representative of his financial backers and not his constituents. Attempts to restrict campaign spending have so far been largely unsuccessful.

The real victims of this are the minorities, who feel that neither of the two major political parties adequately reflects their interests. Alternative party politics are very difficult to finance, and it is virtually impossible to compete with the money of the Democrats and the Republicans in most parts of the country. In any event, the election laws make it extremely difficult for a third (or fourth) party to get on the ballot in many states. This effectively reduces the choices which can be put before the people, and what is usually lost is the vigorous advocacy of minority causes contrary to those of the prevailing political powers and of the vested business interests.

PARTICIPATION AND ALIENATION

Substantial numbers of the American people are excluded from full participation in the economic system and in the political process. On occasions their hopes have been raised by oratory and by the passage of civil rights laws and new social programmes, but the failure of reality to come up to expectation has often deepened the frustration of the poor, the socially deprived, and the politically powerless. They thus resign themselves to the permanence of their existing conditions and sink into apathy, or they become more militant in their demands for equality and justice.

This is the kind of alienation which has happened in the black communities. Their frustration is expressed in militant organisations such as the Black Panthers, in riots, and in a violent hatred of the police. On the college campuses distaste for the Vietnam war and anger at what students see as the inability of 'the establishment' to come to grips with the problems of hunger, poverty, pollution, and so on, led to the demonstrations of the late 1960s. Similarly, the feeling on the part of some whites that the government is insensitive to their distaste for social innovations like school integration has had violent repercussions.

Militancy tends to provoke a 'backlash'. As agents of the established powers, the police and the National Guard have dealt severely with black militants and some student demonstrators, as in the police attack on a Black Panther's headquarters in Chicago, in the treatment of demonstrators at the Democratic convention in the same city in 1968, and the killing of students at Kent State University in 1970. Construction workers, with the American flag on their 'hard hats', have attacked some of the peace demonstrators whom they view as unpatriotic Communist-inspired immoral 'hippies'. Far from being critical of violence against dissent, many Americans approve of it. There is a growing tendency to countenance the use of force, mass arrests, telephone wire-tapping, and the surveillance of individuals suspected of radical political affiliation. 'Law and order' is a current political slogan which can cover a multitude of sins.

American public opinion appears to be polarising about extreme positions. At the one extreme are those whose faith in the nation in unshaken—who see a land of freedom, opportunity, affluence and high moral purpose, with the menace of world Communism, failure to win in Vietnam, rising crime rates, and the unreasonable agitation of Negroes, welfare recipients and radical students as the main clouds on the horizon. At the other extreme are those who see America as a land of oppression, injustice and racism, morally bankrupt, rife with corruption and graft, and controlled by a conspiracy between greedy politicians, big business, and the military establishment. The so-called liberals and moderates occupy the middle ground. The 'silent majority', which has been the subject of much recent political interest as supposedly the custodians of traditional American values, seem to be shifting to the right, or to the conservative end of the spectrum. They now seem less willing to support liberal legislation on civil rights, the rights of the accused, and social programmes, than they were in the middle of the 1960s. This change in attitude, together with the more conservative political philosophy of the Supreme Court following the Nixon appointments, suggests that the next decade is unlikely to be one of rapid reform and social innovation. Some see the need for a period of quiet and consolidation after the changes of the 1960s. Others see a danger that the minorities will be further alienated, setting in motion another round of militancy and backlash.

THE QUALITY OF LIFE

All the issues discussed so far in this chapter have an important bearing on the quality of life. For a long time the Americans have operated on the assumption that national progress could be measured almost entirely in economic terms, by such indicators as income levels and growth of GNP. This attitude is now being seriously questioned. Part of the price of unrestrained economic expansion has been environmental pollution and the under-financing of public services, and the American people are becoming gradually more reluctant to accept this. As increasing affluence is found not necessarily to make people happier, attention is turning to other aspects of the quality of life. In academic and government circles there is now much talk about the need for social indicators, to give a reading on the general well-being of society in the nation and its component parts.

Measuring the quality of life as it varies within the United States is clearly a difficult matter. But some attempt may be made, using statistics relating to many aspects of life dealt with in this book. The following major criteria have been selected as indicative of social well-being:

1. Income, wealth and employment.
2. The quality of the environment, especially housing.
3. Health, both physical and mental.
4. Education, including achievement, duration and level of service.
5. Social disorganisation, or the incidence of social problems.
6. Participation and alienation.

Figures for each of the states for almost fifty conditions relating to the above have been analysed statistically, with the result that it is possible to recognise two major independent dimensions of social well-being. These may be termed *General Socio-Economic Well-Being*, concerned mainly with income, education,

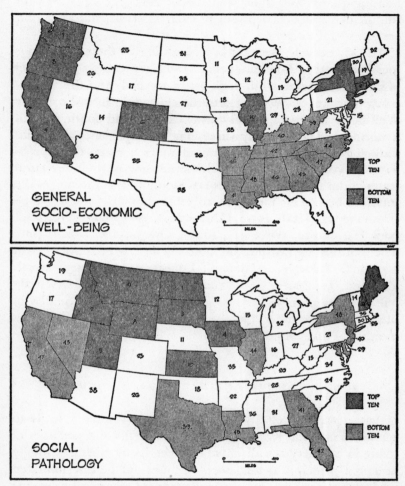

Rankings of the forty-eight contiguous states, on two aspects of social
well-being or the quality of life (based on figures from D. M. Smith,
The Geography of Social Well-being in the United States, MacGraw-Hill,
New York, 1973).

housing quality and so on, and *Social Pathology*, concerned with the incidence of social problems such as crime, narcotics and certain social diseases.

The states have been ranked according to these two major social indicators. Low numbers or ranks represent a good level of social well-being while high ranks are bad, and the accompanying maps show the patterns. General Socio-Economic Well-Being improves steadily away from the old South, in both a northerly and westerly direction. The incidence of Social Pathology is high in the urbanised states because these problems are concentrated in the cities, and low in the more rural states of the plains and the western mountains. A ranking of the states on both these indicators together shows the top ten to be (from the top) Utah, Iowa, Connecticut, Wyoming, Minnesota, New Hampshire, Wisconsin, Idaho, Oregon and Washington. The bottom ten (from the bottom) are Mississippi, South Carolina, Georgia, Alabama, Louisiana, Arkansas, North Carolina, Tennessee, Texas and Florida. This is of course only one of many possible ways to show variations in the quality of life between the states, but the general picture is the same in a number of other similar studies.

SOCIAL JUSTICE AND NATIONAL PRIORITIES

Any discussion of America's problems eventually leads to questions of social justice, or how the benefits and penalties of living in a society are allocated between its members. A widely accepted principle is that people should not be discriminated against, or favoured, by virtue of race, colour, creed or ethnic origin. The observation that particular groups, such as the Blacks or the Jews, are substantially less well endowed with good education, health services, housing and the like than other groups would be regarded as unjust. Differences in treatment between one community or region and others might be looked at in the same way.

To an extreme extent American society distributes the neces-

sities and the good things of life according to the financial
reward the individual gets for his work, as determined in the
market-place. In other words, the Americans generally have
what they can pay for, whether it be material possessions, social
services, status, or political influence. Need is much less important as a distributive criterion, especially when compared with
many nations of western Europe. In America the emphasis is on
the satisfaction of wants which are backed up by economic
and political power, rather than on the satisfaction of basic
human needs.

These issues are raised to try to express some of the questioning which is going on currently in America concerning basic
national values and priorities. While many Americans still
appear to be satisfied that they live in a just society with proper
priorities, a growing minority seriously doubt this. They would
like to see the balance of internal political power shift away from
big business and towards the socially deprived. And in foreign
policy they would like to see a shift away from the aggressive
pursuit of national economic interests, and towards more aid to
the under-developed world with no strings attached. Current
arguments that they should concentrate on putting their own
house in order and let the rest of the world take care of itself
for a while suggest the possible emergence of a new isolation-
ism, which cuts across party political lines.

Whether they think about national problems or simply react
to them, the Americans are now a puzzled people in some
important respects. They are seeing traditional values assailed
by the young, as they reject the material prosperity which their
parents worked so hard for and seek escape in hippie communes
and hallucinatory drugs. They are seeing some of their sacred
institutions challenged, and their deficiencies clearly exposed.
They have recently seen their military might thwarted by a
small Asian nation—a profound threat to their collective masculinity. They see their hard-earned money taken in taxes to
support students who burn the flag in their protests, and on
welfare for Blacks who reject white society. They see their
money spent in foreign aid to nations who show their

ingratitude by failing to support American policy and national interests.

They recognise that they have some critical tasks to perform at home and a vital world role to play. But they seem unsure as to what these are. Their past shows what they can do when they set their minds to it—when they establish a national objective such as to be first on the moon and really work for it. The difficulty now is in deciding just what should be done as the nation and the world changes, and here the pragmatists seem impotent while the visionaries are nowhere to be found. Setting new national courses requires above all political leadership which can inspire the nation towards the true realisation of some of its grand ideals. The absence of such leadership may be the greatest problem of all.

These, then, are the Americans. They are a people with a distinguished history, yet one marred by slavery and social injustice; with the oldest democracy in the world, yet one which is still far from perfect; with enormous natural riches, yet endangering them by thoughtless exploitation of the environment; with the greatest of modern industrial economies, yet unable to keep millions of its people from poverty; with a highly advanced scientific technology, yet failing to provide adequate housing, transportation and medical care for all; with an eagerness to make sacrifices in the defence of free people the world over, yet sometimes unable to distinguish freedom from oppression. In short, like any people, they have their strengths and their weaknesses, their greater qualities serving to accentuate their shortcomings. They are a people who have achieved so much in such a short time, yet still have so much to achieve.

9

Hints for Visitors

CHARTER flights and reduced trans-Atlantic air fares make the United States more accessible to European visitors than it once was. Air travel is now decidedly cheaper than sea, and of course much quicker. Connecting flights to most parts of the country can be boarded in New York, Boston, Washington, and other airports of entry, and there are direct flights to Chicago and other major cities beyond the east coast.

Travel inside the country offers a number of alternatives. The cheapest way is by bus, with Greyhound the major carrier. Students from overseas can obtain a Greyhound ticket for $99 prior to arrival, which gives unlimited travel for three months. These buses are fast and comfortable, and connect most towns and cities. Railways are often less convenient, because of the cut-backs in passenger services in recent years, and they can be almost as expensive as air travel. For businessmen or those without financial constraints air travel is best; by European standards it is relatively cheap and the services run efficiently except in times of bad weather. Car hire is common and very convenient, but quite expensive: major company rates are now (1972) $14 a day and 14 cents a mile with petrol included. For short trips in the city taxis are generally needed, because of the inadequacy of public transportation.

For the tourist, car travel is by far the most convenient and flexible way to get about. Unless the visit is very short, the hire or purchase of a car would be recommended for those who can afford it. Petrol (gasoline) prices are lower than in Europe, but the high consumption of the large American car evens out the cost per mile. American roads are good and usually straight, and an average of 50 or 60 mph is normal except for in-town driving. Covering 300 to 500 miles a day, long distances can be travelled in a relatively short time.

Roadside motels provide instant accommodation all over the country. At the time of writing, the better-quality national chains charge around $10 or $12 a night for a single bed and perhaps $16 to $20 for a room with two double beds (no food included), but rates can be considerably higher in resort and popular vacation areas at the height of the season. Rates in the larger city hotels are comparable. However, comfortable rooms can be found for less in the smaller and older owner-operated motels and in some downtown hotels, particularly in places by-passed by the Interstate highways. Hotel and motel rates are almost always quoted on 'European plan', which means meals not included; with meals it would be 'American plan'.

Breakfast in an average restaurant would cost $1 to $2. Lunch or dinner would vary from $1 for hamburger and chips or a sandwich to $5 or $6 for a good steak. A family of two adults and two children would need at least $35 a day for comfortable motor touring just to cover accommodation, food and petrol, and many American families would allow over $50. But by using a car with low petrol consumption, camping, and preparing their own food, the same family might manage on under $20.

European visitors inevitably find the United States expensive. It is unwise to travel without a reserve in cash or travellers cheques, for unexpected contingencies such as motor repairs, car hire and extra nights in hotels can quickly mount up. Because of the extremely high cost of medical care, visitors with health problems should bring their own medicine or drugs if possible, and health insurance is a sensible precaution for anyone.

Most American businesses have their share of 'fast-buck operators', and visitors should be wary of these. In making major purchases of goods or services, it is sensible to take advice on who are the reliable firms or people to deal with, particularly in the big city. Money can often be saved by shopping around, whether it be for food, toilet requisites, motel rooms, or dental treatment.

Almost every purchase in the United States except for personal services has state sales tax added to the marked price, and this should be allowed for in calculating what will actually be paid for supermarket goods, meals, or hotel rooms. This tax is from 3 to 6 per cent in most states. When tipping, 10 to 15 per cent is in order in restaurants, and 25 cents per bag for hotel or airport porters, but to avoid black looks it should be remembered that anything less than a dollar bill is small change.

Allowance is made for children in almost all hotels, motels and restaurants, and cots, high chairs and even children's menus can be expected. Travelling with children is thus easier than in most countries. However, public lavatories, or 'restrooms' as the Americans delicately call them, are often hard to find (these authors once saw a sign on the New York State Turnpike reading 'Rest Rooms 52 miles'). Visitors should bear this in mind.

In summer most parts of the United States are hot and high humidity can make heat uncomfortable, so lightweight clothing is essential. In winter it can be bitterly cold in all parts except the west coast and the South, so a heavy coat is needed. Tweeds and woollens are fine for outside in cold weather but inappropriate inside, even in winter, because houses, shops and offices are often centrally heated to temperatures which Europeans sometimes find too high. Except for the most formal social gatherings, almost anything can be worn without being conspicuous, for dress is generally casual. Because of the fast cleaning and laundry services to be found both inside and outside hotels, visitors can travel with a small wardrobe.

Visitors should try to avoid coming to the United States with fixed preconceptions, for more often than not they will confuse rather than clarify the experience. And they should certainly not make hasty judgements on the basis of their first encounter with a New York taxi-driver or an under-tipped hotel porter. Some of the big cities can be exciting if disturbing, but the

L

tourist in search of beauty and tranquillity should leave them as soon as possible. Some of the grandest scenery in the world awaits the visitor, especially in the National Parks.

As individuals, the Americans are warm and friendly. Christian names are quickly used, both with friends and business associates, and social life is generally very informal. Some of the friendliness is superficial—a product of a mobile people who have to establish new social relationships quickly—but when friendships firm up they can become deep and lasting.

Whatever the reason to visit the United States, a memorable and exciting experience is virtually guaranteed.

Index

171